CÉCILE DUBOIS

BRUSSELS ART NOUVEAU

PHOTOS | SOPHIE VOITURON

WALKS
IN THE CITY CENTER

CÉCILE DUBOIS

BRUSSELS
ART NOUVEAU

PHOTOS | SOPHIE VOITURON

LANNOO

BRUSSELS, THE BEST CITY FOR ART NOUVEAU

While other cities could probably also lay claim to this title, it is true that Brussels is probably one of the few European cities where the Art Nouveau style has such a prominent presence. This is where the first Art Nouveau buildings were built. That said, things might have been very different. After World War II, several of the innovative masterpieces of architects such as Victor Horta and Paul Hankar were demolished or even thoroughly altered, much like the work of several lesser known architects. Fortunately, people gradually rediscovered Art Nouveau over the years. At the same time, we must remain vigilant! While the interest of Art Nouveau is almost unanimously recognised, many minor heritage elements may potentially disappear, either because of negligence or ignorance. A guide like this one therefore continues to be crucial for raising public awareness about the richness, diversity, and relevance of Art Nouveau as a creative movement, in early twentieth-century society.

This publication contains nine walks, during which you can discover the many facets of Art Nouveau in architecture in various Brussels neighbourhoods. It discusses the personalities of several key architects and decorative techniques used to introduce art into the streetscape. The book also contains several portraits/interviews of owners, conservators, and restorers, who help safeguard this exceptional heritage.

◂ Saint Cyr house, square Ambiorix 11, Gustave Strauven, 1900

INTRODUCTION

▲ Sgraffito, home of the architect Paul Hankar, Rue Defacqz 71, 1060 Saint-Gilles

At the end of the nineteenth century, Brussels architects reacted against academicism, which inevitably led them down the path of Art Nouveau. Victor Horta, with his organic style, and Paul Hankar, whose style was more geometric, created a style of architecture that would soon become internationally famous. In just fifteen years, from 1893 onwards, hundreds of Art Nouveau buildings were built across the capital; initially by the great innovators, and subsequently by their pupils and followers, who were also inspired, in the early twentieth century, by the Viennese Secession and by other trends in European Art Nouveau.

Some of these architects designed *gesamtkunstwerke*, overseeing every aspect of the design, from the architecture to the technical features of a modern edifice (heating, electricity, pipes...) down to the interior decoration and the furnishings. The concept of the 'portrait house' was also developed, designing a house entirely to the specifications of a client.

Initially, Art Nouveau perfectly fulfilled the ambitions of the industrial, often progressive, and free-thinking bourgeoisie. At the time, Belgium was the second industrial power of the world. These clients wished to assert their influence in the city with this new and often exuberant architecture, with its clearly visible metallic structure and with rooms that invited light into the house. Gradually, the style became more democratic, culminating in the construction of Art Nouveau school buildings, social housing, town houses, warehouses, community centres, and so on. While Art Nouveau incorporated industrial materials such as iron and cast iron, it also relied heavily on the artisanal tradition for stonework, woodwork and joinery and ironwork, stained glass windows, sgraffito and colourful ceramic decorations.

In the early twentieth century, Horta already moved away from Art Nouveau, revisiting more classic styles of architecture. Paul Hankar died prematurely in 1901 whereas Henry van de Velde and Octave Van Rysselberghe, two other pioneering architects, pursued international careers. The 'second generation', comprising Ernest Blerot and Gustave Strauven, whose style was more floral, or Léon Sneyers and Paul Hamesse, who developed a more rational architecture, in the vein of Paul Hankar, took over at the helm from the innovators. And finally, there were other notable architects such as Jean-Baptiste Dewin, Paul Cauchie, and Victor Taelemans, who developed their own very personal styles.

The construction of the Stoclet Palace, between 1905 and 1911, by the Austrian architect Josef Hoffman, marked the end of the history of the Art Nouveau movement in Brussels with a masterful flourish. The geometric shape of the Stoclet Palace ushered in the architecture of the interwar period, and would go on to influence several Brussels and international architects. World War I signified the demise of this architecture, which at times was outrageously decorative. Sometimes people even forgot that the pioneers sought first and foremost to rethink spaces. A long period followed, during which Art Nouveau was maligned and forgotten. Some major buildings were demolished, such as Horta's Maison du Peuple, which was built in 1895, in spite of international protests. Fortunately, some buildings were listed and restored ... slowly the tide turned thanks to the visionary insight of people such as Jean Delhaye and Guy and Léo Dessicy. The Horta Museum opened in 1969, just four years after the demolition of the Maison du Peuple.

Nowadays, the style is widely appreciated, garnering the interest of Belgian and international visitors alike.

We must remain vigilant however. The avidity of real estate developers and ignorance can cause irreversible losses. In Brussels, residential Art Nouveau buildings can be found in the bourgeois communes of the first tier—Forest, Saint-Gilles, Ixelles, Saint-Josse-ten-Noode, Schaerbeek, which extend the city of Brussels to the northeast—, which grew exponentially in the early twentieth century. The city seemed to be perpetually evolving. New neighbourhoods were built and the architects who also served as real estate developers and even contractors did not have to go far to find clients for their buildings. In the city centre, where people went for retail and leisure, the programmes were more diverse, but the buildings were also more scattered. They were built in places where there was still some space left in the early twentieth century, or where the town planners decided to create space.

Art Nouveau is never the only style in a specific neighbourhood. It always exists alongside other contemporary styles such as neoclassicism, the first architectural style used when the city expanded to the suburbs, in the 1860s, as well as other 'neo' styles (neo-Renaissance, neo-Gothic, etc.) and eclecticism, which drew heavily on various styles. Art Nouveau also existed alongside the first Beaux-Arts style buildings, which became a prominent feature in Belgian cities from 1905 onwards, and which referred to the French eighteenth-century styles.

It would have been interesting to add an Art Nouveau trail for the communes in the second tier, but this would have been a very long trail, which would have been impossible to cover on foot. When you leave the city centre for Uccle, Watermael-Boitsfort, or Berchem-Sainte-Agathe, you run into several surprising Art Nouveau buildings, which we decided not to include here, as they are often isolated and are sometimes not even visible from the street.

▼ Stoclet Palace, avenue de Tervuren 279-281, Woluwe-Saint-Pierre (Josef Hoffmann, 1905–1911, listed on 13 October 2005). Added to the UNESCO World Heritage List in 2009.

FIRST WALK

THE ORIGINS OF ART NOUVEAU
FROM HÔTEL SOLVAY
TO THE HORTA MUSEUM

Avenue Louise, which was built in 1864 and which constitutes the starting point of this walk, fulfilled a double ambition: to create a new and elegant avenue, which connected the city centre with La Cambre forest and promote a new upper middle class neighbourhood.

A progressive bourgeoisie, drawn to the Art Nouveau buildings in the surrounding area, relied on such innovators as Victor Horta and Paul Hankar for the design of their homes. This walk focuses on the 'manifesto' houses of the Brussels Art Nouveau style and includes three Horta buildings, which were added to the UNESCO World Heritage List in 2000.

◂ Detail of the front door, Rue Forestière 40, Ch. Sée, 1909

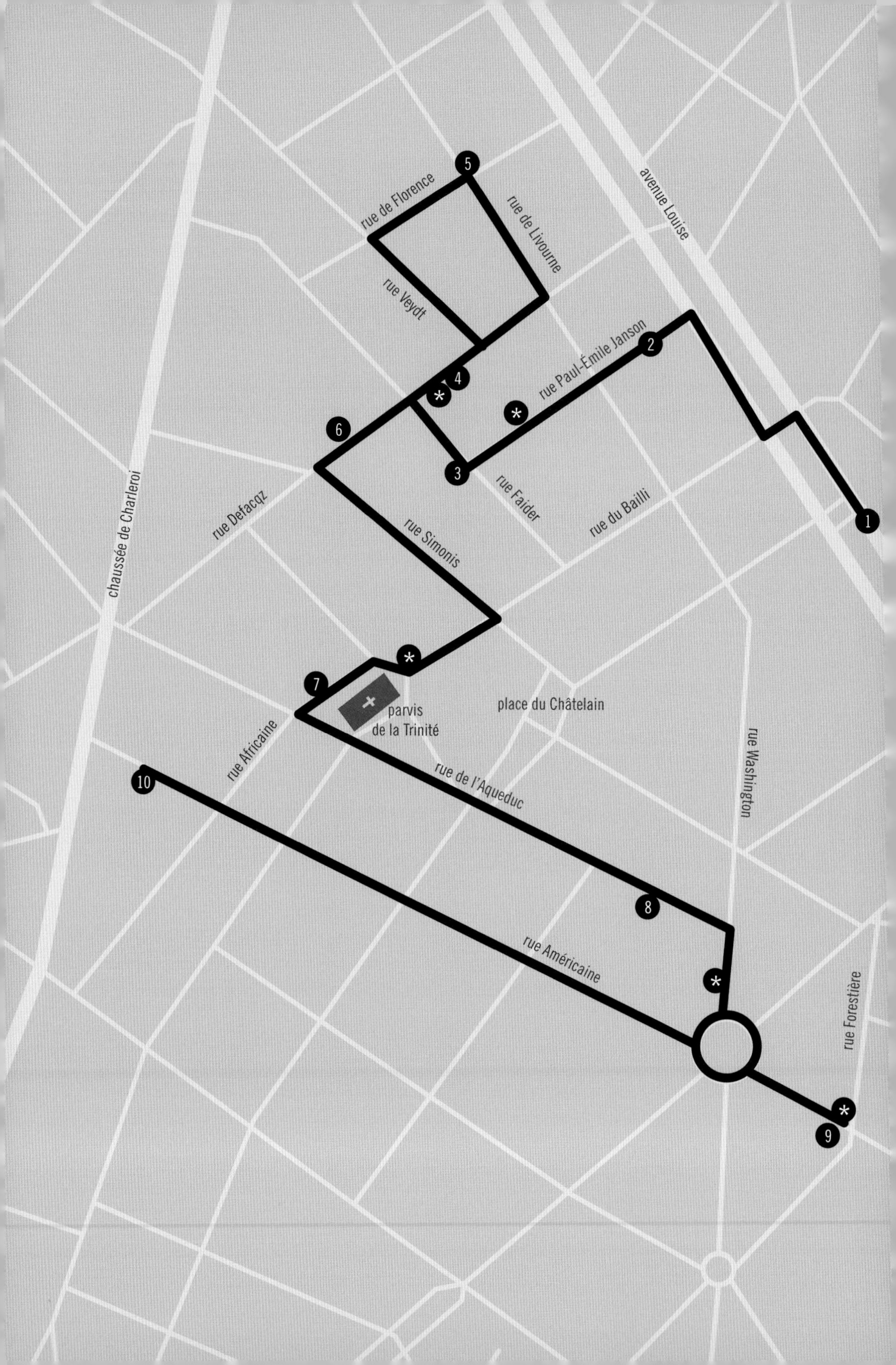
rue de Florence
rue de Livourne
avenue Louise
rue Veydt
rue Paul-Émile Janson
chaussée de Charleroi
rue Defacqz
rue Faider
rue du Bailli
rue Simonis
place du Châtelain
parvis
de la Trinité
rue Africaine
rue Washington
rue de l'Aqueduc
rue Américaine
rue Forestière
1
2
3
4
5
6
7
8
9
10

01 **HÔTEL SOLVAY**
AVENUE LOUISE 224, 1050 BRUSSELS

02 **HÔTEL TASSEL**
RUE PAUL-ÉMILE JANSON 6, 1000 BRUSSELS

03 **HOUSE**
RUE FAIDER 83, 1050 IXELLES

04 **HÔTEL CIAMBERLANI**
RUE DEFACQZ 48, 1050 IXELLES

05 **HÔTEL OTLET**
RUE DE FLORENCE 13, 1000 BRUSSELS

06 **HOUSE AND STUDIO OF THE ARCHITECT PAUL HANKAR**
RUE DEFACQZ 71, 1060 SAINT-GILLES

07 **HOUSE**
RUE AFRICAINE 92, 1060 SAINT-GILLES

08 **HOUSE OF SANDER PIERRON**
RUE DE L'AQUEDUC 157, 1050 IXELLES

09 **HOUSE AND STUDIO OF THE ARCHITECT ADRIEN BLOMME**
RUE AMÉRICAINE 205, 1050 IXELLES

10 **HOME AND STUDIO OF VICTOR HORTA / HORTA MUSEUM**
RUE AMÉRICAINE 23-25, 1060 SAINT-GILLES

1/ HÔTEL SOLVAY

AVENUE LOUISE 224, 1050 BRUSSELS

Architect: Victor Horta

1895-1898

Listed: 7 avril 1977 et 22 avril 1999

Added to the UNESCO World Heritage List in 2000

▲ Dining Room of the Hôtel Solvay

Around the 1890s, Armand Solvay (1865–1930) took over at the helm of the family company which his father, Ernest Solvay, founded in 1863. Solvay invented the industrial process for the manufacture of soda. In 1894, Armand Solvay tasked Victor Horta with the design of his mansion. Horta, who had shot to fame after building Hôtel Tassel, would go on to write in his *Mémoires*: 'In effect, I was welcomed in this environment because in being so bold as to choose me, a sign of energy and independence, Solvay's choice contained, albeit in a different form, the energy that the Solvay brothers needed to invent their soda.'[1]The architect had an almost unlimited budget at his disposal and his relationship with his clients was remarkable, as 'this was an amicable relationship, underscored by the intelligence and charm of his wife, who fortunately was more open to modernism than her husband',[2] even though there were some signs of impatience by the end of the project. Construction commenced in 1895, and while the structural work was completed in 1898, the Solvays ended up having to wait until 1903 before the last furniture was delivered. But the result was unparalleled: this was Horta's masterpiece, the pinnacle of his architectural ideas.

The mansion's design is revealed in the organisation of the façade, which is fifteen metres wide. Horta used white and blue stone, interrupted by lateral oriels on the various floors, enlivening the façade's design and creating the illusion that the central span is hollow. The ground floor is on the street level 'so the master of the house has an office where he can conduct private business and large cloakrooms that connect with the entrance hall and the utility rooms.'[3] A monumental double staircase, with a massive stained glass skylight made of American glass and a painting by Théo Van Rysselberghe, titled 'La lecture dans un parc' (1902) provides access to the reception rooms on the first floor. There are no load bearing walls here. Instead the visible metal structure allows the architect to create wide-open spaces that open out onto one another. On the street side, the reception rooms run across the entire width of the house. At the back of the house, on the garden side, Horta created a dining room and study. All the spaces interconnect, with glazed partitions that can be opened or closed. A second stairwell, also with a stained glass skylight, leads to the second floor, where the parents sleep. The landing has been converted into a veritable conservatory, in the heart of the house. The third floor is where the children and the governess sleep. The servants' quarters are located in the attic, which can only be accessed by the service staircase. Before World War I, the Solvay family employed about a dozen servants.

Horta pushes the principle of *gesamtkunstwerk* to its limits here, designing every aspect of the interior decoration and the furnishings, using only the most valuable and noble materials, including twenty-three different types of marble and seventeen varieties of wood, including several types of African wood. The house is one of the few Horta designs where the original furniture was preserved. If we were to merely limit ourselves to discussing the interior, this would not do justice to the architect, who incorporated it into an original structure, while also seeing to all the technical details: a forced air heating system, electric lighting, and so on. In 1944, the stained glass window on the first floor was destroyed by the impact of the explosion of a V1 bomb. In 1957, the Wittamer-De Camps family acquired the mansion from the Solvay family, transforming it into a sewing workshop and exhibition gallery. Since then, the window and the mansion have undergone several restorations, a process that continues today. The building is only exceptionally open to visitors and is also used for the organisation of smaller events, for conservation purposes.

2/ HÔTEL TASSEL

RUE PAUL-ÉMILE JANSON 6, 1000 BRUSSELS

Architect: Victor Horta

1893-1894

Listed: 18 novembre 1976

Added to the UNESCO World Heritage List in 2000

The year 1893 is an important date in the history of Art Nouveau. This was the year in which Victor Horta built Hôtel Tassel, the manifesto of his organic Art Nouveau style and in which Paul Hankar launched the geometric Art Nouveau style when he built his own house. Emile Tassel, who was employed as an engineer at Solvay, lived with his grandmother and enjoyed receiving friends. He liked to conduct scientific research at home, and was a professor at the Université Libre de Bruxelles. He asked Horta, whom he knew from the Masonic lodge les Amis Philanthropes, to design him a house for a single man. The very balanced façade gives a hint as to the edifice's interior organisation. It is made of blocks of white stone, from Euville and Savonnières, both in the Lorraine region in France, which the Art Nouveau architects preferred to use. By positioning the entrance door in the middle of the façade, Horta already gave a hint of what was to come. Here nothing would resemble anything people had seen to date. In traditional Brussels houses, the entrance door was on the side of the house, in a narrow span. On the upper floor, the salon, dining room and veranda were all located in the main span. On the right and left of the entrance, two small windows light up a parlour and a small hall, which led to the service corridor that gave out into the kitchens in the cellar on the garden side of the house. In the mezzanine, small windows with stained glass panels, which are separated by five slender stone columns with bases and capitals that have been carved to resemble claws, gripping an iron lintel, allow light into the smoking room. On the first floor, light flows into the office through the large window of the bow window with its distinctive iron structure. Finally, the house also had a large study on the uppermost floor.

The façade was divided vertically into three sections. The central spans gradually opens up to the light, while the windows of the two lateral spans become narrower. The small openings on the upper floor are

▲ Stairwell of Hôtel Tassel

even reminiscent of loopholes. The bow window, which protrudes from the façade, has a very organic shape.
The house was very deep (more than twenty metres) and is subdivided into three parts: an area for intellectual life, in the front of house, a rear part, and a central part with a conservatory in the heart of the house on the left, with a skylight and the stairwell on the right, which led to the upper floors, and which had a stained glass skylight above it. The edifice folds back unto itself on this central section, which bathes in natural light and which is the heart of the house.
At the back, the upper floor comprises a succession of rooms, inclusing the sitting room and the dining room. The bedrooms of Tassel and his grandmother were located at the back of the other floors. In the interior, the decoration blended in seamlessly with the structure, as part of the house's general concept. The heart of the house, on the ground floor, was completely open and the metal structure clearly visible, which anchored the interior. The capitals of the cast iron columns extend into tendrils and twists at the crown, creating a whiplash motif that is also used elsewhere in the interior. The floor is decorated with marble mosaics, in white, orange, and green, in organic flame and scroll shapes. The doors and some of the windows have stained glass panels, featuring marine scenes or flowering bulbs. Finally, the wall of the stairwell features a large mural, in gradients of green and orange, with stylised arabesques and plants, attributed to Henri Baes.
After Tassel died in 1920, Norine Couture occupied the premises, after which it was renovated several times. The house was acquired in 1976 by Jean Delhaye, who admired Horta and restored it. Soon after, it was listed. Nowadays it is used as office premises.

Victor Horta (1861–1947) was born in Ghent. He first studied at the Academy of Fine Arts in his city of birth, then spent a year in Paris, and finally ended up at the Academy in Brussels. He then acquired extended work experience in the practice of Alphonse Balat (1818–1895), the architect of Leopold II, who was a figurehead of the classic style, at the time when Balat was tasked with the construction of the greenhouses of the Palace at Laeken. His early projects already bear testimony to his skill in designing classic compositions (the pavilion of the Human Passions, 1890–1899). In 1893, he created his first Art Nouveau style building, building Maison Autrique, followed by Hôtel Tassel. From then on, Horta would develop his own original spatial concept and a new decorative language, drawing on plants for inspiration. Until 1914, he created several gesamtkunstwerke, for a progressive clientele. He also built department stores, Brugmann Hospital (1906), the House of the People (1895), and so on In 1913, he was appointed as Director of the Academy of Fine Arts in Brussels, where he proceeded to reorganise the educational programmes. After World War I, he gave his spatial expression even more free rein, designing the complex structure of the Centre for Fine Arts (1922–1928). During this period, he mainly accepted public commissions, evolving from Art Deco into a simpler more functional architectural style (Central Station, 1937–1952). In 1939 and 1945, he burnt most of his archives. He did leave *Mémoires*[4], but never completed them. Four of his buildings have been added to the UNESCO World Heritage List.

Hôtel José Ciamberlani at 23–25, Rue Paul-Émile Janson, is currently undergoing restoration. It was built by Paul Hankar in 1897 for the brother of Albert Ciamberlani (listed on 7 June 2001).

3/ HOUSE

RUE FAIDER 83, 1050 IXELLES

Architect: Albert Roosenboom
1900
Listed: 7 December 1981

After working in the practice of Victor Horta, Albert Roosenboom (1871–1943) built several Art Nouveau buildings before becoming one of the greatest champions of the Beaux-Arts aesthetic, which was so similar to eighteenth-century French architecture.
This façade, built in white Silesian bricks, accentuated by white stone from Savonnières and metal elements, rests on a tapered blue stone base. The scraper has been installed in the base, into an interlacing moulding, which connects to the letterbox. The moulding extends upwards, transforming into the console for the bow window. The curved bow window is very similar to that of Hôtel Tassel, with its visible metal structure. A small balcony sits on top of it, its wrought iron railing curving outwards and its shape reminiscent of a fish trap.
On the top floor, the windows are surrounded by an exceptional sgraffito, which is in dire need of restoration, and which is attributed to Privat Livemont. In the centre of the composition, a woman's face, eyes closed, the index finger resting on her lips, invites the spectator to be silent as the owners of the house sleep behind these windows. Two chubby putti, on either side, hold poppies, flowers that are known among others for their sleep-inducing properties.
Golden stars twinkle higher up.

4/ HÔTEL CIAMBERLANI

RUE DEFACQZ 48, 1050 IXELLES

Architect: Paul Hankar
1897
Listed: 12 janvier 1983

This striking geometric Art Nouveau façade has two large horseshoe-shaped windows on the first floor and some extraordinary examples of sgraffito. The entire building was restored in 2006 and is among the best-preserved houses designed by Paul Hankar.

It was built by Paul Hankar for the Widow Ciamberlani, who commissioned it for her son, the Symbolist painter Albert Ciamberlani (1864–1956). In 1927, the architect Adrien Blomme radically redesigned it, adding a garage.

The twelve-metre wide façade, made of white brick from Silesia, with bands of white stone from Euville, demonstrates great freedom in the distribution of the windows. There are four openings on the ground floor, two on the first floor, and seven on the upper floor.

On the first floor, in front of the horseshoe-shaped bay windows, with wooden frames (with several divisions) a balcony extends across the entire façade. It is supported by five consoles, the central one being the most expressive. The wrought iron railing repeats the same floral motif seven times, a reference also to the shape of the large bays.

Sgraffito plays a crucial role in the façade's composition. Here the work was done by Adolphe Crespin, Hankar's associate, after a drawing by Ciamberlani. Claire Fontaine restored the sgraffiti in 2006, which by then were very degraded. The composition centres on a large pear tree, throughout the seasons, whose branches fan out across the entire width of the façade. This tree is associated with allegorical characters, symbolising the stages of life. Spring to the right, during which the pear tree blossoms provide a joyous sight for the small child held by its parents. Summer can be found in the centre, where a child picks flowers while a man lights a torch with another torch, the symbol of transmission. A couple of peacocks sit in the tree, symbolising immortality and renewal. To the left, a bearded old man symbolises winter, caught in the northern wind, turning his back to the tree which has lost its leaves.

The medallions of the entablature frieze, under the cornice, feature hunting scenes—Ciamberlani was a hunter—, symbolising modern times and the expulsion of archaic forces.

The entrance opens onto a staircase, which leads to the upper floor, which is well above the ground floor. To the right, several rooms succeed each other: the sitting room, the dining room, and the veranda.
Unlike Horta, Hankar chose to respect the traditional floor plan of Brussels houses, seeking to draw in natural light at the back of the house instead. His verandas generally featured a large bay window, and were partly covered by a glass skylight, to let in the light. While the sitting room has a distinct Louis XVI feel to it, the dining room is all Art Nouveau and has been restored to its former style.
The furniture, which was designed by Hankar, is now exhibited in the Design Museum in Ghent.
The monumental square stairwell has a glass skylight. On the first floor, at the front of the house, a huge sitting room extends along the entire width of the building, letting in the light through two horseshoe-shaped bays in the façade.

At 50, Rue Defacqz, the appearance of Hôtel Janssens, which was built in 1898 by Paul Hankar for a painter friend of his, has been thoroughly altered. Originally, the right span, which was the widest, did not extend above the imposing bay window, with a glass skylight above it, letting the light into the painter's studio. In 1904 and 1908, the building was raised (by Maurice Van Ysendyck and subsequently Adrien Blomme). As a result, the height of the spans was reversed (listed on 12 November 1998).

PORTRAIT: CLAIRE FONTAINE

Claire Fontaine conserves and restores murals and is a decorative painter, specialising in the study and restoration of decoration and ancient techniques. She graduated from the École de Recherche Graphique (ERG) and the Van Der Kelen Institute, as well as studying at the École d'Avignon and the Centre for Conservation of Architectural Heritage of San Servolo in Venice. For eight years, she studied the restoration of the painted interiors of Venetian villas and historical dwellings in Italy and elsewhere in Europe. From 1997 onwards, she dedicated herself exclusively to the restoration of murals in Belgium.

Cécile Dubois: You seem to prefer Art Nouveau buildings, intervening on various levels. Can you give us some examples of your work?
Claire Fontaine: In the Horta Museum, I restored oil glazes and the gilding of the railing of the stairwell. In Maison Autrique, I restored the floral decorations of the linoleum, as well as reconstructing old Japanese wallpapers in the main salon of the Quaker House.

CD: Ultimately, when one does finally get to visit these interiors, it is not immediately evident that you have worked there.
CF: That's right! A restoration effort above all is about conservation. We spent four months cleaning and fixing the murals and ceiling paintings of Hôtel Max Hallet, without really being able to show what we did.

CD: How do you go about restoring an element that no longer exists?
CF: If the element is sufficiently documented with archive photos or there are sufficient traces of the original, I try to reproduce the figurative elements, as well as the intention, the instant of creation. You must focus on the technique, the gesture, and time it took to create this, and the matter and original colours, which you must try to reconstruct.

CD: Another aspect of your work is the restoration of sgraffito works. One of your most striking interventions is the restoration of the sgraffiti of Hôtel Ciamberlani. But you have also worked on Hôtel Otlet, on houses built by the architect Blerot and on the sgraffiti of Privat Livemont. How is the restoration of sgraffito different from the restoration of murals in interiors?
CF: The sgraffito on the façade can be seen from a distance and are part of a set of unique and irreplaceable elements that enhance each other, like the ironwork and the stained glass windows.
When I stand on the scaffolds between the sky and the street, I can see all these elements close

▲ Claire Fontaine restoring a sgraffito at 76, Avenue Sleeckx in Schaerbeek

up, and most of the time, I can see a lot, at least when it's not raining! The sgraffiti are permanently exposed to the elements. So my efforts will be more far-reaching than for an interior.

CD: What is the main thing you concentrate on when undertaking conservation or restoration?

CF: I think that a building's aesthetic is mainly determined by its coherence. The most intelligible, the most harmonious polychromy is the original one, of the building and its decoration, from the outset. So you must often undertake historical and stratigraphical research to find the original under 100 years of layers of paint. The analyses and studies I conduct before any restoration project are crucial in this framework. An intervention is never neutral. It leaves a new and datable material trace, which is related to the time of the job and the profession of restorer, which constantly evolves. As a specialist, I must limit my intervention to the strict minimum, avoid any irreversible interventions and must not compromise future treatments and analyses. When working in monuments that people live in, I must sometimes try to strike a fine balance, facilitating the daily life of the building's occupants while adhering to restorer's code of conduct. While the conservator/restorer has a great responsibility vis-à-vis the creator and the public, I often think of the owners as the custodians of the artwork. We share the same task, namely to hand down these masterpieces to future generations and must do everything necessary so they can enjoy these works and feel the emotions that these works inspire as long as possible. It pains me to see historical buildings that are not maintained or have been altered.

5/ HÔTEL OTLET

RUE DE FLORENCE 13, 1000 BRUSSELS

Architect: Octave Van Rysselberghe, working with Henry van de Velde
1894-1898
Listed: 6 May 1984

This town house is worth the detour if only for the personality of the owner who originally commissioned it. Paul Otlet (1868–1944) was a doctor of law, a militant socialist, a visionary, and a pacifist. An avid bibliographer, he established the Office international de Bibliographie and in 1905 developed the Universal Decimal Classification System, which is still used in libraries today. He also took the initiative for the Palais Mondial or Mundaneum, which aimed to gather all the knowledge of the world in one place. This tireless worker spent all his earnings on his research, and already had a glimmer of what the Internet could be, in the early twentieth century: 'Here, the desk has no books on it. Instead there is a screen and a telephone within hand's reach. There, in the distance, is a large building, which contains all the information and all the books. [...] The answer to the question asked by cordless or cord telephone is then projected on the screen.'[5]

In 1894, Otlet tasked Octave Van Rysselberghe with the construction of a private family home, on a large corner plot. The complex composition of the façade, with its many recesses and projections, reveals something about the elaborate organisation of its interior. On Rue de Livourne, the house has a separate artist's studio in a duplex. The blue stone substructure contrasts with the façades in stone from Savonnières and Euville.

There is only one continuous sgraffito under the cornice, which repeats a pattern of shells and arabesques, adding a dash of colour to the façade.

The entrance, in Rue de Florence is recessed, and is crowned by a monumental stained glass window, in which the fluid style of Henry Van de Velde is very recognisable. Van Rysselberghe commissioned the interior decoration and furnishings from him. The interior is organised around a large central mezzanine, which is illuminated from above. The main stairwell is built

around this and gives access to the various rooms on various levels.
The dining room is located on the ground floor, to the left of the hall, and has a bow window on the corner, which is very expressive. It connects to the kitchen in the cellar with a dumbwaiter. A few steps lead up to the sitting room, whose windows overlook Rue de Livourne. A large family sitting room is separated from Otlet's study, with screens, on the courtyard side, and is extended in the bow window in the right span, on the side of Rue de Florence. The bedrooms and bathrooms are on the upper floor.
A large part of the town house's decoration has been preserved, including a mosaic floor and several stained glass windows.
Nowadays a law firm occupies the premises.

Octave Van Rysselberghe (1855-1927), the older brother of the painter Théo Van Rysselberghe, started to build houses that were inspired by the Italian Renaissance, after studying architecture at the Academy of Fine Arts in Ghent and spending two years studying in Italy. At the end of the 1880s, he stopped working as an architect, choosing to grow grapes in Overije for a few years instead. He returned to architecture at the time that Art Nouveau emerged as a style, developing his own personal version of it. He subsequently built several buildings on the Belgian coast, more specifically in Westende, where he was hired as an architect by the Compagnie Internationale des Grands Hotels Européens. Horta considered him one of 'his most interesting and most independent fellow architects'[6]. Van Rysselberghe ultimately moved to Saint-Clair on the Côte d'Azur in the south of France.

A multitalented creator and a European well before the term was coined, **Henry Van de Velde (1863–1957)** was a major personality in the history of twentieth-century art. A renowned painter, Van de Velde turned to the decorative arts, hoping to design practical and beautiful everyday objects that could also be reproduced. In 1895, he built the Bloemenwerf, his own home in Uccle. Its rational design expressed his desire to reject any ornaments that were inspired by styles from the past. As the interior decoration commissions started to pour in, Van de Velde founded his own production company in 1899. In 1900, he moved to Berlin where he was appointed as artistic adviser to the Grand-Duke of Saxony-Weimar in 1902 who tasked him with the revival of the art production industry in the region. Between 1904 and 1911, he built the School of Fine arts in Weimar and his school of decorative arts (which would go on to become the Bauhaus in 1919). Its educational programme was founded on the immediate cultivation of a sensibility in students rather than focussing on the study of styles. In 1926, he returned to Belgium where he founded and directed the Higher Institute of Decorative Arts at La Cambre. He is considered one of the driving forces behind the Belgian architectural avant-garde.

6/ HOUSE AND STUDIO OF THE ARCHITECT PAUL HANKAR

RUE DEFACQZ 71, 1060 SAINT-GILLES

Architect: Paul Hankar
1893
Listed: 26 May 1975

The home of Paul Hankar, which was built around the same that Horta built Hôtel Tassel, is also considered an Art Nouveau manifesto. Hankar and Horta explored radically opposite paths in the visual arts and aesthetics, but this did not prevent them from appreciating each other's work. In Horta's buildings, the bow window is developed in a very organic manner, whereas here, the oriel (which protrudes from the façade on several floors) seems to have been grafted onto the façade. Its profile is accentuated by slender blue stone columns that rest on very high consoles. The façade of Hôtel Tassel is almost monochrome, whereas Hankar's façade stands out because of the original polychromy. Horta almost exclusively used white stone, which was expensive, whereas Hankar's projects, which often were designed for artists who were less well off, meant that he could not use expensive materials. That is why Hankar combined bricks in different colours with stone, adding sgraffito to the façade for decoration.

The red brick façade, which has been enhanced with blue and white stone, rests on a base of blue stone and red pudding stone rubble. The sgraffito in a Japanese style by Adolphe Crespin complete the façade's decoration. The sgraffito of the entrance span lists the year in which the house was built, surrounded by hydrangeas. The sgraffito of the oriel, which is combined with geometric ironwork, represents cats against a backdrop of nasturtiums that wind their tendrils up the façade. Under the cornice, four small sgraffiti under arches symbolise the different times of the day: morning (the pigeon), day (the pigeon and the sun), evening (the swift) and night-time (a bat and a starry sky).

The ironwork is also very refined, especially the guardrail of the terrace, which serves as a support for the two wrought iron columns that support the largely overhanging cornice.

Inside, the house is organised according to a traditional floor plan, except for the square stairwell, which develops in the façade, above the entrance. Currently, the house is subdivided into apartments.

Paul Hankar (1859-1901) was born to a family of craftsmen specialising in stonework. After graduating with a diploma in architecture from the Academy of Fine Arts in Brussels, where he became interested in the renewal of the formal language which inspired the artistic avant-garde, Hankar worked for the practice of Henri Beyaert (1823–1894), from 1879 until 1892. Here he learnt to create an architecture that was characterised by constructive rationalism, favouring the visible use of materials, inspired by Eugène Viollet-le-Duc. In 1893, he paved the way for a new form of architecture, while building his own home. The language of this style was not in any way similar to the historicising vocabulary but was instead based on a constructive logic and the nature of the materials used. This kicked off a very busy career, building town houses, private dwellings, artist's studios, country houses, commercial premises, exhibitions (the Congo exhibition in Tervuren in 1897), and furniture sets. His premature death marked the end of his research, which influenced many of his students, including Léon Sneyers and Paul Hamesse.

At 6, Parvis de la Trinité, on the corner of Rue du Bailli, an eclectic building, which is visibly inspired by Art Nouveau, stands out because of the ceramic tile façade, with decorative ceramic panels on the uppermost floor, in which you can make out swifts. On the corner, the decoration continues with a medallion with a woman's profile.

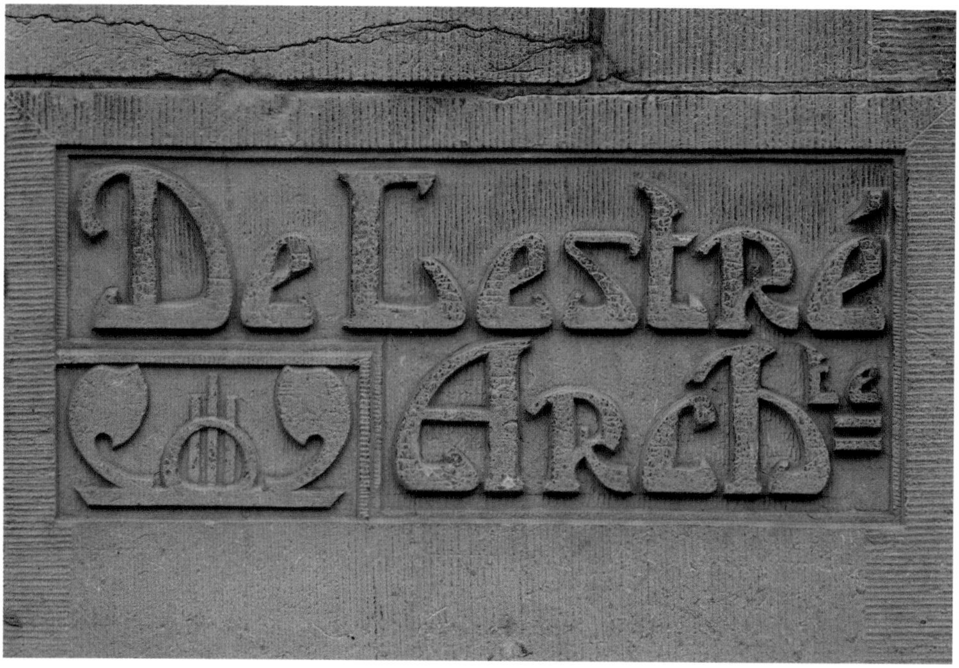

▲ Signature of the architect Benjamin De Lestré

7/ HOUSE

RUE AFRICAINE 92, 1060 SAINT-GILLES

Architect: Benjamin De Lestré-de Fabribeckers
1905
Listed: 4 December 1997

This geometric Art Nouveau façade, with its single span, has a bow window on the first floor. Its console runs down all the way to the base, with an overhanging terrace, which protrudes over a horseshoe arch. A curved cornice rests on top of the three windows on the uppermost floor, with a circular arch that is similar in form to the second-floor bay window.

The façade's verticality is accentuated by the two slender columns that flank it, and which rise up from the first floor extending into the pinnacles.

There are several elements that enhance the quality of the façade: the architect's signature, in a very Art Nouveau script, the wooden window frames, the wrought iron elements, and the metal lintels, above the bays on the ground floor with their geometric decoration.

A decorative element is repeated several times, in the wrought ironwork and in the stonework: a circle intersected with horizontal lines above three stylised branches, a pendant that is similar to elements of Paul Hankar's work and the style of the Viennese Secessionists.

The influence of Art Nouveau is only apparent in the façade and in some elements of the interior design, especially in the entrance hall and the stairwell. Each of the other rooms has a specific style, from the Flemish neo-Renaissance to the Empire style.

After graduating from the École Saint-Luc in Ghent, **Benjamin De Lestré (1865–1928)**, who often used his wife's name, de Fabriebeckers, started building houses in a geometric Art Nouveau style, which was influenced by the Viennese Secession. In 1908, he switched to Beaux-Arts architecture.

8/ HOUSE OF SANDER PIERRON

RUE DE L'AQUEDUC 157, 1050 IXELLES

Architect: Victor Horta
1903
Listed: 19 February 1998

The discreet decoration of the façade is part of the structural work. Just look at how the blue stone elements have been sculpted. Interestingly in this work by Horta, the majority of the façade is built in red and white bricks, the combination of which adds a polychrome and decorative feature to the façade. Quality ironwork and some bronze elements such as the door handle complete the decoration.

The façade, which has been kept very simple and is even rather traditional in terms of composition has a large bay under a metal lintel, which draws natural light into the study.

Even though the floor plan is rather traditional, Horta still devised this project as a *gesamtkunstwerk*, combining architecture and decoration into one entity: a mosaic floor in the entrance hall, a beautiful handrail on the main staircase, doors with stained glass windows, integrated furnishings, original door handles, and so on.

This house is still a single family dwelling today.

The Vinck House at 85, Rue Washington (1906) is evidence of this return to simplicity in Victor Horta's work in the early twentieth century. Another floor was added to the coated façade, with blue stone elements, in 1927 by Adrien Blomme. Émile Vinck (1870–1950) was a doctor of law and a member of Les Amis Philanthropes. He was affiliated with the Belgian Workers Party and was elected a municipal councillor for Ixelles in 1904.

The writer and art critic Sander Pierron (1872–1945) was a friend of Victor Horta and would support him throughout his career in the articles he wrote. Born to a modest family, he left school at the age of thirteen to work as a typographer. He loved art and beauty and taught himself all about it. Horta designed an affordable house for him, which was less costly than the houses he usually built, because he wanted to cater to a less wealthy friend. The design is simpler but nonetheless interesting as a result.

9/ HOUSE AND STUDIO OF THE ARCHITECT ADRIEN BLOMME

RUE AMÉRICAINE 205, 1050 IXELLES

Architect: Adrien Blomme
1908
Listed: 5 June 1997

The first home and studio of the architect Adrien Blomme is a house with a very eclectic style, which was influenced by Art Nouveau but which also references the English *Arts and Crafts* movement. At the start of his career, Blomme already demonstrated a penchant for corner plots, which required him to devise innovative spatial solutions. Two long red brick façades, with white stone elements, rise up on either side of the corner. The façades have bow windows and bay windows with different shapes, with wooden window frames, and stained glass windows or coloured glass. The garage replaced the study in 1929. The corner where the main entrance is located is monumental: it has a curved gable, with a terrace with a stone railing. The house's original subdivision and interior design scheme have been retained. The monumental stairwell is built on the corner, and can be seen in the façade, with windows on either side of the entrance span, whose sills punctuate the staircase as it winds its way up the house.

Adrien Blomme (1878-1940) has left an impressive legacy in Brussels, with urban blocks, apartment buildings and villas combining Art Nouveau, Art Deco, and the neo-Baroque. He was very active during the period between the two World Wars receiving many commissions from the Wielemans brewery family.

The entrance door of the eclectic house (Ch. Sée, 1909) at 51, Rue Forestière, on the corner of Rue Américaine, is worth the detour. Its bronze handle features a draped woman with lovely undulating tresses, as well as two decorative red copper panels.

10/ HOME AND STUDIO OF VICTOR HORTA/ HORTA MUSEUM

RUE AMÉRICAINE 23-25, 1060 SAINT-GILLES

Architect: Victor Horta

1898

Listed: 16 October 1963

Listed as a UNESCO World Heritage Site in 2000

In 1898, Victor Horta, who was regarded as an established architect by then, designed the plans for his private house and studio. While the two adjoining houses have different façades, they are subtly united by the materials used, namely Euville limestone and Savonnières stone. The house's façade, to the left, with its varnished oak entrance door, is enhanced by a bow window, with a balcony. Its railing is reminiscent of a butterfly's wings. Three metallic braces connect the first-floor balcony with the bow window's stone consoles, winding their way up the stone. The glass floor of this balcony protrudes above the entrance, creating a small protective canopy. Once again, the architect demonstrates his ability to combine different materials—here stone and metal—without disrupting the design's flow. The workshop's façade is more austere and has large windows. The entrance door is made of pitch pine. To the right, a large bay window (restored) lets natural light into the cellar and the ground floor. On the first floor, the bay window to the left is divided by a slender column that rests on an elegant sculpted stone. The air vents have been integrated in its base. On the top floor, an industrially manufactured window lights up the designers' studio.

Nicknamed the 'archisec'[7] by fellow members of the masonic lodge, for his cutting opinions and replies, Horta never worked alone. In 1900, just before moving to Rue Américaine, Horta employed 'sixteen designers, two painters, and two sculptors'.[8] This workforce may seem disproportionate if you consider the number of projects—about fifteen—he was overseeing at the time. But he was very consistent in his methods, working like a master architect, designing the architecture, the technical aspects, and the interiors of all his projects. Horta drew even the smallest details, often spending several days at a time in his studio and only resting for a few hours. These sketches were then redrafted by a designer before Horta made the last corrections. Then plaster scale models were created from the designs. Prototypes of certain furnishings were first built in cheap wood. The architect never reused any of his models, creating new and original work for each project. While this was a time-consuming approach, it also proved prohibitively expensive! Sometimes his designs for façade stones were so complicated that the workmen in the quarries were unable to follow his instructions. In that case, the moulding workshop produced these elements in plaster first, on a life-size scale, as a model. It is easy to see how this culminated in delays on some projects, causing conflicts with his contractors. The interiors of the house-workshop are separate entities, even though they are connected. The design is built around three stairwells: the stairwell of the square floor area of the house around a light shaft, the staircase of the workshop, and the servants' staircase. The spaces in the living quarters are situated on alternating levels. Horta designed the interior decoration and the furniture, to perfectly match the architecture, down to the last detail.

In 1906, after his divorce, Horta increased the floor area of the buildings on the side of the garden. Perhaps he intended to build an apartment on the second floor for his daughter Simone. In 1919, upon his return from the United States, he sold the house and studio to different owners.

In 1961, the municipality acquired the house, at the insistence of Jean Delhaye, transforming it into a museum that opened in 1969. It subsequently acquired the studio, in 1973, so the museum could be extended. The two units were restored in several phases, initially by Jean Delhaye, later by Barbara Van der Wee. The house was furnished with original furniture, when found, and with other work by the architect.

At the end of 2016, the museum was expanded to no. 27 rue Américaine, a house built by Jules Brunfaut in 1900. The museum's reception area was installed in the house, to reduce the burden of visitors on Horta's building.

The architect **Jean Delhaye (1908–1993)**, who trained under Victor Horta, spent a lot of his time and money, from the Fifties onwards, working on preserving his master's work. He pushed for the conservation and the restoration of the Tassel, Dubois, and van Eetvelde houses as well as Horta's own house and studio. While he was unable to prevent the demolition of Maison Aubecq (1950) and the Maison du Peuple (1965), he did however save large sections of these two buildings. In 1991, Jean Delhaye, who was able to recover plenty of documentation and furniture, among others from Horta's widow, established a foundation with his wife Renée. Its archives will be kept in the Horta Museum. Brussels Art Nouveau is certainly indebted to Delhaye.

PORTRAIT: FRANÇOISE AUBRY

Françoise Aubry is an art historian. In May 1976, fresh out of school, she was employed at the Horta Museum as assistant to the Curator in Chief. She was appointed to this post herself in 1981. Over the past forty years, she has seen the public's attitude to Art Nouveau change. She also assisted in the restoration of the museum, from 1989 until 2014 by the architect Barbara Van der Wee. At the end of 2016, she hopes to open the extension of the museum, which will have a new reception space and exhibition gallery.

In 2018, Françoise Aubry will retire, but she will continue to work on projects related to Art Nouveau. Because, whereas Horta was passionate about architecture, Françoise Aubry has always nursed a passion for Art Nouveau.

Cécile Dubois: How did you become the Curator of the Horta Museum?

Françoise Aubry: During my studies, I wrote a dissertation on the influence of the Arts and Crafts movement[9] on Henry van de Velde when he was building the Bloemenwerf. At the time, I found it very difficult to find a professor at the ULB who would accept to supervise a dissertation on a theme related to Art Nouveau. Finally, the architect Victor Martigny accepted this task. I particularly liked the fact that Van de Velde built his own house, that he designed all the objects in it, and that he wanted everything in it to be beautiful. I was very impressed by this desire for beauty. I mainly liked the floral, naturalist motifs of the Arts and Crafts movement. I lived in the country until I was eighteen years old and in Brussels I felt like I was clinging on to the world of nature, plants, and animals in one way or another. Art Nouveau was an art form that observed nature and used it as a leitmotif.

After graduating, I worked for the publisher Marc Vokaer for a few months. He was the first to publish works about Victor Horta. Then Victor Martigny invited me to apply for the position of assistant curator at the Horta Museum. I was interviewed by Mr Delhaye, who was the museum's director at the time, who in essence said the following at the end of our meeting: 'I think you'll do, but there can be no question of you doing any work on Van de Velde in the future!'. Mr Delhaye believed that only Horta existed!

CD: What does your job as Curator entail?

FA: I manage the finances, the workforce ... I don't write here because I'm interrupted too often. The restoration of the house took up a lot of my time. Jean Delhaye had conducted a first restoration phase in the 1960s. By the end of the Eighties, it became obvious that a second restoration was needed. We first developed a master plan to define the objective of the restoration. It took almost twenty-five years to complete!

CD: What did you enjoy the most during your career as Curator?

FA: Working with Barbara Van der Wee, the architect who restored the museum and working with the craftsmen. I loved talking to these professionals. These are people with a brain that works and with hands that produce—the best of both worlds. We looked for them, and selected them. Many of them were excellent artisans, but were not familiar with Art Nouveau. They became specialists, while working with the architect Barbara Van der Wee, who is very precise, who appreciates a job well done, and who can be very demanding. She listens and takes what people tell her into account. She develops her projects by talking to the people who will execute them. I have always argued in favour of learning programmes, especially work placement programmes or work-learning programmes. These artisans are gradually becoming extinct. And yet these are magnificent professions, with which you can earn a good living.

CD: Is it difficult to make a house like this one accessible?

FA: This house was built for a family of three, not to receive 67,999 visitors a year, as was the case in 2014. We had to strengthen the stairwell in 1990, as it had started to shift under the cumulative weight of all the visitors. The floors suffer wear and tear, and so do the mosaics, the parquet, and the murals. We deal with rather substantial problems on the conservation level. The museum's extension will help reduce some of the damage. The direction of the visit will change. Visitors will walk up via the central staircase and walk down again via the service staircase. This means visitors no longer cross each other in the stairwell, relieving the pressure on the structure of the main staircase.

CD: Which Art Nouveau work has a special place in your heart?

FA: I love Horta in general, but I am really passionate about the work of Mackintosh,[10] about his apartment buildings, his watercolours, and his drawings of flowers, his place in the city of Glasgow, his life, and his relationship with his wife. Horta expressed himself as an artist in his murals, in his mosaic designs, but Mackintosh really expressed something very intimate and personal in his watercolours. Horta always has the rigour of the architect whereas Mackintosh is much more whimsical, his work is much more fragile. I am infinitely enamoured with his art.

52

SECOND WALK

IXELLES, SAINT-GILLES AND FOREST

FROM HÔTEL HANNON
TO THE PARK OF FOREST

A walk that criss-crosses lovely avenues to explore artist's studios or the homes of architects, but which also includes several social housing complexes that were built in the early twentieth century.

◂ Social housing, rue Marconi 32, Léon Govaerts, 1901

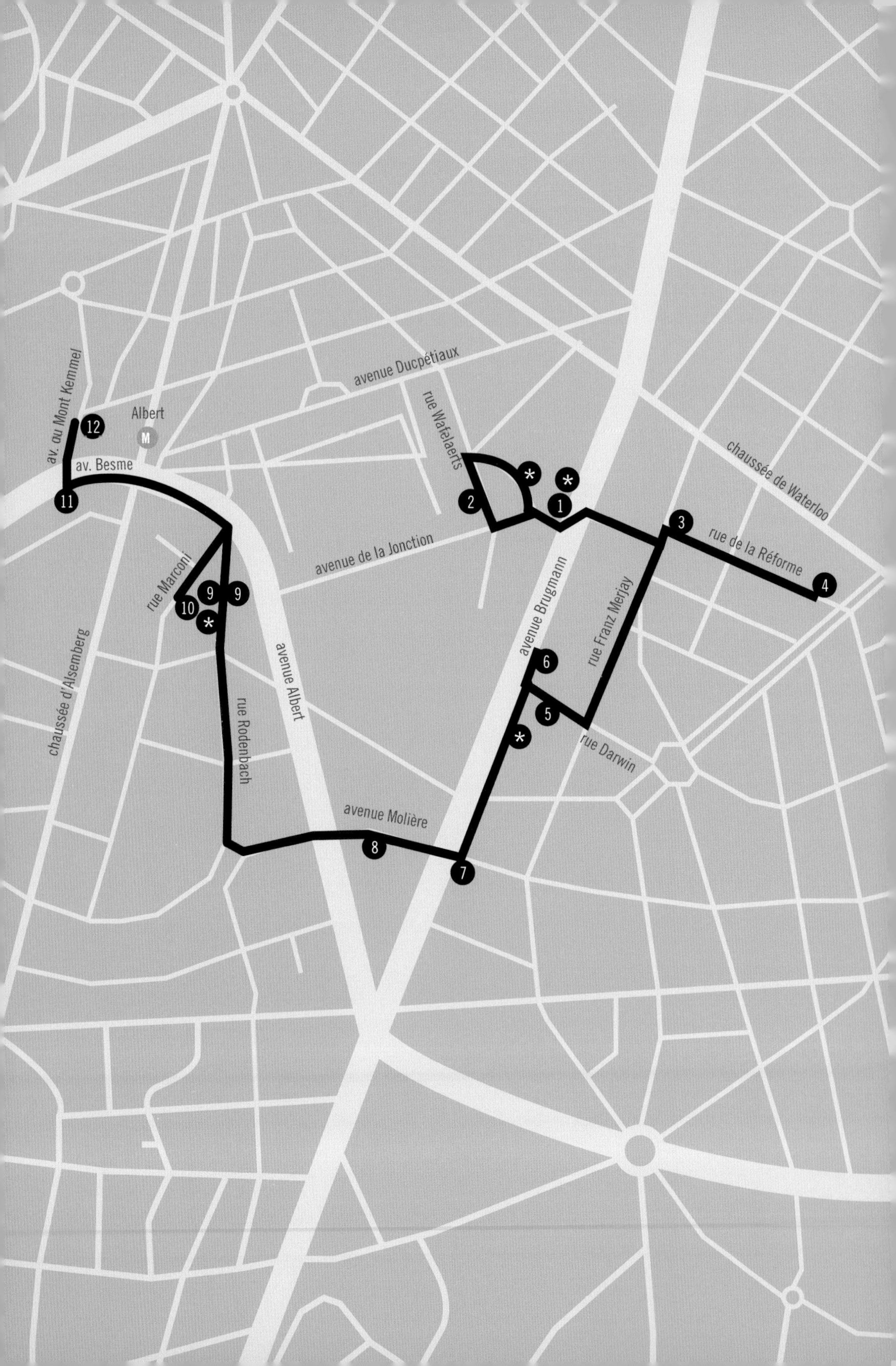

avenue Ducpétiaux
rue Wafelaerts
av. au Mont Kemmel
Albert
M
av. Besme
chaussée de Waterloo
rue de la Réforme
avenue de la Jonction
rue Marconi
avenue Brugmann
rue Franz Merjay
avenue Albert
chaussée d'Alsemberg
rue Rodenbach
rue Darwin
avenue Molière
1
2
3
4
5
6
7
8
9
9
10
11
12

01 **HÔTEL HANNON**
AVENUE DE LA JONCTION 1, 1060 SAINT-GILLES

02 **CLINIC OF DOCTOR VAN NECK**
RUE HENRI WAFELAERTS 53, 1060 SAINT-GILLES

03 **HOUSE AND STUDIO OF THE PAINTERS GÉO BERNIER ANDJENNY HOPPE**
RUE DE LA RÉFORME 4, 1050 IXELLES

04 **HOUSE AND STUDIO OF THE PAINTER GEORGES LEMMERS**
RUE DE LA RÉFORME 74, 1050 IXELLES

05 **HOUSE AND STUDIO OF THE PAINTER LOUISE DE HEM**
RUE DARWIN 15-17, 1190 FOREST

06 **HOUSE AND STUDIO OF THE SCULPTOR FERNAND DUBOIS**
AVENUE BRUGMANN 80, 1190 FOREST

07 **GROUP OF BUILDINGS COMPRISING HÔTEL VANDENBROECK AND TWO TOWN HOUSES**
AVENUE BRUGMANN 176-178 ET AVENUE MOLIÈRE 177-179, 1190 FOREST ET 1050 IXELLES

08 **HOUSE OF THE ARCHITECT JEAN-BAPTISTE DEWIN**
AVENUE MOLIÈRE 151, 1190 FOREST

09 **SOCIAL HOUSING**
RUE RODENBACH 14-22 ET 29-33, 1190 FOREST

10 **SOCIAL HOUSING**
RUE MARCONI 32 ET 34-36, 38-42, 1190 FOREST

11 **VILLA**
AVENUE BESME 103, 1190 FOREST

12 **VILLA BEAU-SITE, HOUSE OF THE ARCHITECT ARTHUR NELISSEN**
AVENUE DU MONT KEMMEL 5, 1190 FOREST

1/ HÔTEL HANNON

AVENUE DE LA JONCTION 1, 1060 SAINT-GILLES

Architect: Jules Brunfaut
1902
Listed: 18 November 1976 and 29 November 1983

The Hôtel Hannon is an exceptional work of art in several aspects.

It was commissioned by Edouard Hannon (1853–1931), who worked as an engineer at Solvay. He started out working in the company's branch in Dombasle, near Nancy, before travelling extensively as a technical director. In 1907, he was appointed CEO of the company, a position he held until 1925. He was very wealthy and counted several progressive artists and intellectuals among his friends, who also influenced the design of his home. Hannon was married to Marie Debard, the daughter of the Mayor of Dombasle. The couple had a daughter, Denise, who was born in 1880. He chose Jules Brunfaut (1852–1942) as his architect, who trained as an engineer at the Civil Engineering College of the University of Ghent, and then went on to study architecture at the Academy of Brussels. He subsequently worked under Henri Beyaert, who specialised in neo- styles. During his career, he designed around one hundred townhouses, villas, utility buildings, and exhibition pavilions in the typical Flemish Renaissance style, and subsequently in the Italian Renaissance style. It seems he accepted to work in the Art Nouveau style here, combining it with eclectic elements for the interior decoration scheme, as a friend of Edouard Hannon. This Art Nouveau design is the only such design he ever made.

The house was inhabited until Denise died, in 1965. It then remained vacant and vandalised for many years, at a time when Art Nouveau was no longer considered relevant. In many cases, buildings were demolished and other masterpieces irrevocably transformed. The house was acquired by the municipality of Saint-Gilles in 1979, and restored from 1984 until 1989. Until 2014, it was the home of the Contretype photo gallery. In addition to hosting exhibitions that focused on the work of contemporary photographers, Contetype also highlighted a more personal aspect of Edouard Hannon's life, namely his passion for photography. Hannon was a talented amateur photographer and the founding member in 1874 of the Association Belge de Photographie. At the time, this art form was just emerging. Hannon brought back many sociological and documentary photos from his journeys, which were also aesthetically pleasing. At the end of 2014, Contretype moved and the Hotel Hannon was restored again.

The building's location, on a large and wide corner plot, is reminiscent of other older houses such as Hotel Otlet (Octave Van Rysselberghe, 1894) or Hotel Aubecq (Victor Horta, 1899). For the façade, Brunfaut combined blue stone for the base with white limestone from Euville and white Silesian bricks. It has a hipped gable roof on both sides, with a pediment and a large bas-relief by Victor Rousseau (1865–1958) on the top floor, called 'La Fileuse', an Allegory of Time.

The façade on Avenue de la Jonction is more expressive. Its main section, which recesses considerably on the upper levels, has a lovely bow window on the upper level, with glass windows behind which the conservatory was located. The façade is extended to the left, by a wall that connects the house with the stables, which have since been demolished.

The entrance door has a transom above it, with a stained glass window with stylised floral motifs. Its umbel-shaped handle already offers an indication about the furniture that awaits us behind the door. Once inside, a tiny hall with marble panels leads into a majestic central hall, after you walk up a few diagonally arranged steps. The majestic central hall has a dome painted with stylised flowers and bordered with a frieze of oak leaves and acorns. Around the hall, on the 'bel-étage' level, Brunfaut has arranged the dining room, the conservatory, the smoking room and the sitting room. A winding staircase leads to the first floor, where the rooms, the bathroom, and dressing room are located.

The house is surprising because of the amazing array of decorative elements. The wrought iron railing of the stairwell, the stained glass windows by Raphaël Evaldre, the mosaic floors, and the frescoes by the painter Paul-Albert Baudouin (1884–1931) in the smoking room and stairwell. Edouard Hannon contacted Emile Gallé (1846–1904) for the luminaires and the furniture. The latter was a master glassblower and the founder of the Ecole de Nancy. He also commissioned furniture from Louis Majorelle (1859–1926), a talented designer. Nowadays the furniture can be found in various museums, including the Musée des Arts Décoratifs in Paris, the Musée de l'Ecole in Nancy and so on.

Alongside the Hotel Hannon, the façades of n°s. 51, 53, and 55 are all that remain of these houses along Avenue Brugmann, which were built in 1883, 1895, and 1899 respectively. The interiors were replaced in 1980 by social housing, comprising nineteen apartments and studios. A small courtyard garden now connects the gardens of the three houses with that of the Hotel Hannon. No. 55, a geometric Art Nouveau house designed by Edouard Pelseneer, is striking because of its original bay windows with Moorish arches and the sgraffito works by Paul Couchie. Its name, 'Les Hiboux' or 'The Owls', was inspired by the sgraffito that sits atop the entrance but also by the owls sculpted into the blue stone, which cover the pinnacles and the dormer window (listed on 27 October 1983). Edouard Pelseneer (1870–1947), whose family had a long-standing tradition of working as self-employed woodworkers, regularly collaborated with Horta. This was his first job as an architect.

At 24 Rue Félix Delhasse, a magnificent Art Nouveau house (Emile Lambot, 1905) was definitely influenced by Victor Horta. The façade has a fluid design and a bond of layers of stone and faux stone. The central entrance door is flanked by two slender consoles that constitute the consoles for the bow window. The original window frames have yellow glass sidelights with Japanese style transoms.

▲ Hôtel Hannon
▲ House, 24, Rue Félix Delhasse

2/ CLINIC OF DOCTOR VAN NECK

RUE HENRI WAFELAERTS 53, 1060 SAINT-GILLES

Architect: Antoine Pompe
1910
Listed: 7 December 1981

From 1890 to 1910, Belgian architecture tried to break away from the pastiche and the neo-styles, which the upper middle classes so enjoyed, with Victor Horta and Paul Hankar leading the charge. This movement gave rise to new masterpieces, but culminated in a dazzling array of charming buildings in which the decorative aspect often took priority over the building's form and function. The clinic of Doctor Van Neck, which Antoine Pompe built in 1910, was a decisive step in the evolution of the city's architecture.

'The novelty of the shapes, the simplicity of the lines, the new use of certain materials [...] all pointed to position taking, creating controversy among an audience that was not accustomed to such bold positions.'[1] This minimalist and rational design is a turning point and a harbinger of the architecture of the period between the two World Wars. In 1910, M. Van Neck, who had just graduated with a diploma in orthopaedic medicine, commissioned a private clinic from his friend Antoine Pompe. The design includes offices, a waiting room, a gym, and a private apartment. The architect combined a light Denain brick with elements in Euville stone. The metal lintels are clearly visible. Pompe designed every last detail. Monumental columns enliven the façade. They are the ventilation shafts of the various rooms, and therefore have a functional role first and foremost. On the first floor, the large gym extends across the building's entire width. The two large lateral bay windows and the bay window with the transom were originally bordered with glass bricks, which let in the light while also isolating the space behind it against the rays of the sun, noise, and temperature changes. The central balcony is detachable, so large cumbersome objects can be pushed through without having to use the staircase. Light metallic guardrails in front of the large bay windows ensure the window-washers are safe while doing their job.

Nowadays the building is home to the Institut de Rythmique Jaques-Dalcroze.

Antoine Pompe (1873–1980), who was largely self-taught, studied design and applied arts in Brussels and Germany, training in a variety of techniques including engraving on metal, ironwork, design, furniture and flatware design, jewellery, joinery ... and finally architecture! Together with Adhémar Lener, he built the Palace Hotel in Place Rogier in 1908. Doctor Van Neck's clinic was his first own work, which he built at the age of thirty-seven. From 1910 until 1921 he worked with Fernand Bodson on projects that combined an ideological commitment with formal and technological inventiveness. He mainly built villas and small apartment buildings. Although their design is for the most part rational, they still point to the architect's human and sentimental approach to architecture. While Pompe came to architecture late in life, he had a long and distinguished career, living until the ripe old age of 106! He had plenty of fantasy, and verve, and was able to create a lot with very little. He never refrained from expressing his ideas in polemic articles. A tireless inventor, Pompe had several patents in the fields of building and joinery and even invented revolutionary roller skates!

3/ HOUSE AND STUDIO OF THE PAINTERS GÉO BERNIER AND JENNY HOPPE

RUE DE LA RÉFORME 4, 1050 IXELLES

Architect: Alban Chambon
1902
Listed: 3 July 1997

Géo Bernier (1862–1918) was an animal painter who mainly became famous for his paintings of cows and horses. He was also a founding member, in 1893, of the Le Sillon artist's society. His wife, Jenny Hoppe (around 1870–?) painted flowers, landscapes, and interiors. Many critics and art lovers knew their studio very well as Bernier regularly exhibited his work there.
The architect of their home and studio, Alban Chambon (1847–1928) is better known for the enchanting decorations he created for theatres, hotels, and casinos, rather than as an Art Nouveau architect. While a lot of his output no longer exists, you can still see how talented an artist he was at the Hotel Métropole (Place De Brouckère, 1000 Brussels), which he decorated in 1892.
While Alban Chambon designed the house, he tasked his son Fernand (1876–1944) with the construction process. In all likelihood, the architect Paul Hamesse, who worked in Chambon's studio at the time, also contributed to this house, which is very similar in style to the geometric Art Nouveau style that he used at the time.

The beige brick façade, with its orange brick bands, rests on a white rusticated stone base. It is subdivided into three spans, with the third one having one storey more. To the left, the entrance door is capped, on the upper floor, with two rows of narrow, paired windows, which light up the stairwell.
In the centre of the façade, a bay window rests on elaborate metal consoles. Below them, and in the right

span, the windows have decorative borders or friezes. The ironwork features stylised plant motifs.
The building has retained its original floor plan and some of its decorations. It has two studios at the rear, which are oriented to the north, and which have large bay windows and skylights. The largest one, on the ground floor, can be accessed from the entrance hall and leads into an exhibition gallery that was added in 1907. The smaller studio is on the first floor.

4/ HOME AND STUDIO OF THE PAINTER GEORGES LEMMERS

RUE DE LA RÉFORME 74, 1050 IXELLES

Architect: Gabriel Charle
1904
Listed: 18 November 1976

This house, which was built for Georges Lemmers (1871–1944), a popular painter of portraits and landscapes, was sold to the artist Marguerite Mommen Ithier soon after. The architect Gabriel Charle (1868–1919), a former trainee of Henri Jacobs and Georges Hobé, mainly built private homes, in various styles, to the specifications of this clients.
The red brick and white stone façade, on a base of rusticated sandstone, is rather eclectic but features plenty of Art Nouveau elements, including trapezoidal bay windows, sgraffiti, and geometrical ironwork. On the first floor, the bay windows have stained glass windows that were designed by Marguerite Mommen Ithier, in which you can distinguish swans frolicking about in a pond on which water lilies float.
The interior, which is a combination of neo-Renaissance and Art Nouveau, has been preserved. The fireplace in the dining room at the front of the first floor is decorated with a relief that represents a drinking scene. The fireplace in the studio at the back of the house features the motto 'Nulle dies sine linea' ('No day without a line'), a maxim coined by Pliny the Elder and appreciated by artists because it refers to the need to practice one's art daily to achieve perfection.

5/ HOME AND STUDIO OF THE PAINTER LOUISE DE HEM

RUE DARWIN 15-17, 1190 FOREST

Architect: Ernest Blerot
1902 and 1905
Listed: 9 October 1997

There are several artist's residences in this neighbourhood. Louise de Hem (1866–1922), who originally came from Ypres, moved to Brussels in 1886 although she also spent a lot of time in Paris, where she trained as a painter and pastel artist. From the 1890s onwards, she became a popular portrait artist.

The house (at no. 15) and the studio (at no. 17) were built at a three-year interval. The house's façade, which combines white stone with bands of blue stone, is typical of Blerot's immaculate style: the windows were framed with blue stone, the transom windows have stained glass windows, the house has a trapezoidal bow window, and the bay windows on the upper floor have a horseshoe-shaped arch above them, which tapers out into a tympanum in which sgraffiti featuring country scenes have been created. The entrance door, with its transom window with woodwork that radiates out, is somewhat unusual. Usually Blerot preferred to have a stained glass window or a sgraffito in the transom above the entrance door. The ground floor, which has been somewhat altered, still has several of the original elements, including the woodwork, the stained glass windows, mosaics, and so on. The studio's façade, which is completely level, has two tiers of bay windows, through which plenty of daylight falls in. It features a large sgraffito in slightly faded colours, in which a young woman, an allegory of the arts, is drawing by the side of a pond. The studio was subsequently transformed into a house and was renovated in 2006 by the architects Lhoas and Lhoas.

▼ 15, Rue Darwin

6/ HOME AND STUDIO OF THE SCULPTOR FERNAND DUBOIS

AVENUE BRUGMANN 80, 1190 FOREST

Architect: Victor Horta
1901
Listed: 20 July 1972

Victor Horta befriended numerous sculptors on whose services he relies for various projects. They include the sculptor, engraver and medallion maker Fernand Dubois (1861–1939), who trained under Charles Van der Stappen. The façade is organised around a central span, with windows in different shapes, which let light into the stairwell. On the right, the studio has a large bay window, while a balcony on the left is the only element that protrudes from the building. The façade is not built in white stone, as is often the case in Horta's designs. Instead the architect chose to only use blue stone here. As a result, this house is not as exuberant as the master's earlier designs.

The house is organised around the artist's family and professional life, and, as is the case for the architect's own home, around three flows: the main stairwell, the service staircase, and the staircase that connects the various spaces in the studio. In this house, however, the private and professional areas are not separated as distinctly as in Horta's own home (see p. 28). The sewing room, for example, is located in the studio, pointing to the special relationship between Fernand Dubois and his wife 'whom he loved to such an extent that he dared not be separated from her, not even for an instant.'[2] To the right of the main entrance, a small waiting room, which has two small twinned windows, connected the private living space to the professional studio space. The entrance was through the double door on the right of the façade.

Nowadays, the house is occupied by the Embassy of the Republic of Cuba.

Avenue Brugmann was built in 1871 on the initiative of the banker, philanthropist, and landowner Georges Brugmann. It still largely looks as it used to when it was originally built, with buildings in various architectural styles. You can see examples of Art Nouveau at 120, 122, and 124, with houses built by Ernest Blerot in 1904 (which were listed on 30 January 1997). No. 120 is a typical example of the architect's work. The façade's composition is similar to that of Louise de Hem's house (at 15, Rue Darwin). The windows on the upper floors are connected with splayed arches, with sgraffiti with a floral theme, which have been embellished with gold leaf and which have recently been restored. The houses at 122 and 124 look more austere, and are less typical of Blerot's style. Jacques Arets, who published a book on the architect's work, believes that they cannot be definitively attributed to Blerot as a result[3].

7/ GROUP OF BUILDINGS COMPRISING HÔTEL VANDENBROECK AND TWO TOWN HOUSES

AVENUE BRUGMANN 176–178 AND AVENUE MOLIÈRE 177–179, 1190 FOREST AND 1050 IXELLES

Architect: Paul Vizzavona
1908-1910
Listed: 28 June 2001

This group consists of three buildings in an eclectic style, with Art Nouveau elements, namely Hôtel Vandenbroeck, on the corner of the two avenues, in white stone, and two town houses on either side, in light brick. While the three buildings are different, a sense of unity is derived from the ironwork, which is of the same quality throughout. On the side of Avenue Molière, the façades have a small front garden, while the front garden of the mansion on the corner is fenced in by a garden gate, which sits in sculpted Art Nouveau white stone pillars.

The mansion is typical of the style of Paul Vizzavona, who combined French classicism with Art Nouveau. The white stone façade features arched windows and has a large sloped roof, with a four-sided roof on the corner, also called a pyramid roof, which forms a small tower and opens out onto a small terrace that is protected by a wrought iron Art Nouveau style guard rail.

The interior, which has been well preserved despite some alterations, refers to eighteenth-century French architecture, both in the floor plan and the decoration scheme.

While the upper middle classes had no qualms about choosing the Art Nouveau style for the exterior of their houses, they often preferred a different decorative style for their interiors.

The two adjoining houses both have a large balcony with a wrought iron guardrail on the first floor.

Paul Vizzavona (1881–1956) was a French architect who trained at the École des Arts Décoratifs in Paris under Charles Garnier, who created the design for the Paris Opera. He moved to Brussels around 1903–1904, working as a designer in the studio of Victor Horta before opening his own studio in 1906. He designed several houses and apartment buildings or office buildings in a style that combined the elegance of Victor Horta's organic Art Nouveau—Horta even accused him of plagiarism[4] taking Vizzavona to court—and the French classic tradition. In 1914, Vizzavona left Belgium for France, working in the Var region from then on.

8/ HOUSE OF THE ARCHITECT JEAN-BAPTISTE DEWIN

AVENUE MOLIÈRE 151, 1190 FOREST

Architect: Jean-Baptiste Dewin
1906
Listed: 8 November 2007

Jean-Baptiste Dewin's private home sits alongside the impressive Hôtel Philippot (Jules Brunfaut, 1905), whose façade is decorated with a large relief sculpted by Jef Lambeaux. The house was restored in the most expert manner by Francis Metzger of Ma[2]. This house serves as a manifesto for the architect's style.

The verticality of the white stone façade, which is subdivided into two spans, which are divided into three sections on each level, is accentuated by the high and narrow bay windows.

The wood frames are subdivided and feature coloured windowpanes in which you can distinguish three-petalled flowers, which resemble the diaphragm of a camera. The motif is also used in certain parts of the mosaic in the entablature: two large panels, one in each span, in red, black, and gold featuring three-petalled flowers three times, which are surrounded by owls. The wood cornice is punctuated with modillions and slender twinned consoles that extend into slender columns in the entablature. The garden's geometric garden gates have been restored.

In 2005, the house was acquired by new owners, who loved its sleek design, its spaces, and the quality of the stained glass windows. At the time, the house had not yet been listed. It took a lot of work before this slightly outdated house was inhabitable and functional again. When the house was listed in 2007, the owners changed tack, deciding to restore the house to its original state. The interior, which has undergone a renovation in the Art Deco style in 1922, retained many of the original elements but the furniture was unfortunately lost. The restoration was finally completed in early 2014[5].

The hall's decoration scheme combines marble, granite, and marble mosaics. A flight of stairs leads to the upper floor, which is made up of successive spaces. At the front, the owners have created a library in the old sitting room, which leads into the dining room and a veranda that opens out onto the garden. The doors and windows have been decorated with stained glass, some of which feature a pelican motif. The new furniture was built in line with the architecture and decoration scheme of the rooms. During the restoration, the wallpapers were removed layer by layer in these rooms, revealing stencilled wallpaper, which was gradually restored. The wallpaper, which blends in seamlessly with the decoration of the stained glass windows, is similar to the style of Josef Hoffman.

Jean-Baptiste Dewin (1873–1948) was the son of an ornamentalist sculptor, from whom he probably inherited his talent and appreciation for decoration. Dewin specialised in hospital architecture but also built social housing and several town houses, which evolved from a simple and elegant Art Nouveau style, inspired by the work of Paul Hankar and the Viennese Secession, to a more original Art Deco style, with a more complex spatial organisation. During the Twenties and Thirties, he built the town hall of his commune, Forest, which is considered one of the many Art Deco masterpieces in Brussels (2, Rue du Curé, Forest).

PORTRAIT: FRANCIS METZGER

Francis Metzger divides his time between his architectural practice, Ma²-Metzger & Associés Architecture, and his work as a lecturer at the Faculty of Architecture of the Université Libre de Bruxelles. Since 1983, Metzger has received several commissions for contemporary buildings and the restoration of unique buildings. He has already restored the Solvay Library, Maison Autrique, Delune Castle, the Dewin house, and Villa Empain and undertook the restoration of the Ægidium and the Saint Cyr house, where he sat down with us for an interview.

Cécile Dubois: How did you become interested in this restoration project?
Francis Metzger: Restoration projects are like the lottery of life. After I graduated, I was approached about 40, Rue aux Laines, a listed building which became my first restoration project. I was then entrusted with the restoration of the Solvay Library, without really having done very specific studies on the subject. But I had the curiosity, which allows you to develop the skills and, above all, the methodology because of the interest you have in a specific field.

CD: Which is your favourite period in restoration terms?
FM: I don't really have a favourite period. I like works in which you can feel the architect's passion for his work, gesamtkunstwerke, works that are somewhat like those Russian dolls: you start from small to large or vice versa. There is always a sense of coherence, in every direction. In that sense, Art Nouveau and Art Deco give me the greatest joy.

▲Francis Metzger on the roof of the Saint Cyr house

I think that architecture involves a relationship with a place, a programme, and a moment in time. Something always happened beforehand, and something will always happen afterwards. An architect's job is very difficult. You conceive the project, you think about it, you design it, and then you discuss it with your client. Then you work frenetically to obtain a planning permit and complete the building project. During this process, the building's identity is developed. Once the building is completed, you take photos which never portray people. Because the architect knows that people will move in the next day, and that the building will start to lose its identity. In the following years, it will be repainted, false ceilings will be installed, and the rooms enlarged or reduced in size ... The house loses its identity, even to the point of becoming unrecognisable. I call this the tragedy of architects. Finally, a decision must be made as to whether the building will be retained, demolished, or restored. And our work, as an architect-restorer, consists of reclaiming this lost identity.

CD: What do you like so much about restoration?
FM: The conversation with an architect who is no longer there, trying to understand what he was thinking. As a contemporary architect, you are sometimes overcome by doubt and then you find a solution. These architects experienced exactly the same. Once you have understood the architect's signature style, his work becomes like a novel, which is missing the last pages. You have a faint idea about the scenario and you will complete the project, not in his style, but as a contemporary architect, while respecting the coherence of the scenario. That is what interests me the most, to work in resonance with and respect for the architect's work.

CD: Which building would you like to restore in Brussels?
FM: There are two, unsurprisingly. The Stoclet Palace, which is very well maintained however. There is so little to do that my contribution would be relatively modest. The project that is closest to my heart, however, is the Law Courts. In its current state, the courthouse no longer resembles Poelaert's original design. The floor plan has changed and the way the light falls in. This is a major building, a building that defines the landscape of Brussels. Emptying it would have consequences obviously: neglect, vandalism, risk of fire... In any event, it will never be demolished, so its restoration will be three times as expensive. We need to think about this, bring justice back to the courthouse, undertake a real restoration as soon as possible, which will be funded by the rent you will no longer have to pay elsewhere. I think in the long term this restoration will prove to be free.

CD: Can you tell us about some surprises you encountered during the restoration of a building?
FM: There was one recently during the restoration of the Dewin house. I prefer to call it a lost masterpiece as nobody remembered what this house looked like at the start of the twentieth century, because Dewin altered his building as time progressed and also erased any traces of his work. Finding the origins of this building, which was probably one of its most beautiful manifestations, was truly marvellous. All the more so, since the house did not give any hint of what it concealed at the outset ...

CD: Which is your favourite Art Nouveau building in Brussels?
FM: I like many of Horta's buildings, but I think I like his house best, as I think that this is the epitome of a gesamtkunstwerk. Horta has fewer means for this building project but revealed himself to be an outstanding organiser of space and light. I am infinitely moved by this building; besides the spatial aspect, there is also the decorative aspect of Art Nouveau, which I find less interesting. For me, the most interesting buildings are spatially inventive buildings.

9/ SOCIAL HOUSING

RUE RODENBACH 14-22 AND 29-33, 1190 FOREST

Architects: Charles De Quéker and A. Hannaert
1903

During the last quarter of the nineteenth century, Forest, which to date had been more of a garden suburb, underwent intense and unbridled urbanisation. The upper middle classes moved into new houses along the wide, tree-lined avenues—Avenue Molière and Avenue Albert—, whereas the lower classes found houses in the adjoining streets. In the early twentieth century, the Société Anonyme des Habitations à Bon Marché of the Brussels agglomeration built several social housing complexes for blue-collar workers, replacing the old dead-end alleys with affordable housing. The company was founded and chaired by Charles Buls and sought to address the problem of rehousing working-class families that had been driven out of Brussels following the clean up of the city centre. They were relocated outside Brussels.

In 1903, architect Hannaert and Charles de Quéker, who ran the building authority, studied the plans for eight double houses, with three floors, to be built in Rue du Chat, which is now called Rue Rodenbach. What makes these houses so special, is that the stairwells are built on the outside of the building, on the street side, in inflammable materials. They give access to two apartments on each floor, each with four rooms, which give out onto an exterior terrace. This ensemble is a good example of the social housing complexes that were built in the Art Nouveau era, because of the subtle combination of red and orange bricks, which create a nice colour scheme and the interesting combination of volumes, thanks to the protruding stairwells. Originally the stairwells had small pyramid-shaped roofs but these were replaced with platforms for aesthetic reasons around 1929.

At 37–39 Rue Rodenbach, two buildings (1905–1911) catch the eye. One, in white stone, has an inscription on the façade, 'École Communale – Gemeenteschool', and gives access to the former municipal school no. 4 (now called Ecole en Couleur). A long corridor gives out onto a courtyard, around which the classes have been built.

The other building, in red brick, was probably the head teacher's residence. This group of buildings is typical of the style of Henri Jacobs, who specialised in Art Nouveau school buildings. As the working-class population in the neighbourhood grew and more social housing was built, the municipal authorities were also prompted to open a new school (listed on 12 February 1998).

Social housing, 18, Rue Rodenbach ▸

10/ SOCIAL HOUSING
RUE MARCONI 32 AND 34–36, 38–42, 1190 FOREST

▲ Workers' houses, Rue Marconi 34–36 and 38–42

In 1901, the Société Anonyme des Habitations à Bon Marché de l'Agglomération Bruxelloise (the Brussels affordable housing authority) tasked three architects with designing the plans for three double houses, for eight families each. The underlying idea was to give the authority the opportunity to study which approach worked best for building housing for multiple working-class families.

The most original building, without a doubt, is the one at no. 32, which was designed by Léon Govaerts (and listed on 6 November 1997). The façade is organised around the striking entrance door, of Egyptian inspiration, which is flanked by two slender columns, which fan out at the level of the capital, into a wide motif that covers the lateral openings. The same motif, in a simplified version, can also be found above each window. The window frames are arranged at an angle, for better light, and the façade also has a large wood cornice. The floor plan of the housing was considered quite original at the time: an entrance hall, with an inbuilt cupboard, gave access to the rooms at the front and back of the unit. Each apartment had a WC, a kitchen, and a laundry room, which led to a terrace, at the back of the building.

No. 34–36, which was built by Émile Hellemans, who would go on to build the eponymous Cité of the Marolles, is more classical in style.

At no. 38-42, finally, Henri Jacobs, who had already built several social housing complexes for Foyer Schaerbeekois, built an apartment building, whose orange brick façade features several sgraffiti.

The history of social housing is made up of choices, clashes between different models, tensions between partisans of the development of a large number of rental apartments and partisans that favoured homeownership. At the end of the twentieth century, the industrial development of Brussels attracted many families to the city, who set up house near the factories where they worked. The workers' housing was catastrophic: they lived in sordid alleys, in very small housing, in very unhygienic conditions, ad everyone was on top of each other.In 1889, a law about homeownership for the most affluent workers was enacted, marking a first step on the path towards a solution. This legislation promoted the creation of parapublic social housing authorities, which aimed to build, buy, sell, or rent out workers' housing. Around this time, Cité Hellemans was built in the heart of the Marolles (1912), replacing the workers' hovels with several apartment buildings.

After World War I, the lack of housing forced the authorities to adopt a socialist law, in 1919, establishing the Société Nationale des Habitations et Logements à Bon Marché (SNHLBM). Its role was to supervise the local parapublic housing authorities, to promote the creation of new housing authorities, and fund the construction of housing. In the early 1920s, this new impetus gave rise to the construction of many social housing complexes, including garden cities.

11/ VILLA

AVENUE BESME 103, 1190 FOREST

Architect: Alphonse Boelens
1903
Listed: 23 February 2006

King Leopold II wanted a park in Forest, which was subsequently built by Victor Besme and inaugurated in 1882. Along the park, several picturesque villas and terraced houses were built for the upper middle classes.

This villa is one of the most successful designs of the architect Alphonse Boelens (1887–1936). Boelens often worked with and is often confused with his brother Victor (1872–1955), the deputy director of Public Works at the Municipality of Uccle. Alphonse, meanwhile, was appointed municipal architect in Ixelles in 1908. The two architects combined eclectic influences and Art Nouveau in their projects.

Here the Art Nouveau elements are mainly concentrated in the front façade, in the combination of the materials, wood and wrought iron, the decoration of the window frames and the balconies, the sgraffiti, and so on. The façade, which is made of enamelled white stone bricks, punctuated with bands of blue stone, has an overhanging cornice. The design of the bay window on the ground floor is exceptional. Its rounded transom is crowned with a blue stone arch, which connects with the blue stone jambs. This design visually accentuates the rounded shape of the window opening. The stained glass panels in the entrance door have been preserved. The lateral façade features an awning. The house's floor plan is traditional, however, with a stairwell that leads to an upper floor with three successive rooms. The decoration, which has been preserved is completely eclectic.

12/ VILLA BEAU-SITE, HOME OF THE ARCHITECT ARTHUR NELISSEN

AVENUE DU MONT KEMMEL 5, 1190 FOREST

Architect: Arthur Nelissen
1906
Listed: 23 February 2006

Our visit ends with a stunning architectural gem. Its architect, Arthur Nelissen (1878–1922), was born in the Netherlands but studied in Brussels where his parents lived from 1879 onwards. While he built many houses and apartment buildings in the Brussels agglomeration, his own home, which he built soon after getting married, is still his masterpiece.

The rather narrow façade, which is just under five metres wide, is perforated on the first floor by a horseshoe-shaped arch, followed by a tiny loggia. The window that gives out onto this loggia also has a horseshoe-shaped arch. These arches are larger than a half-circle or a half-oval. This feature, which is typical of Hispano-Moorish architecture, is often used in Art Nouveau architecture.

The façade has been covered with white enamelled bricks, but all the window arches are accentuated with green bricks and blue stone. The ground floor, which is built entirely in blue stone, in the Art Nouveau style, has beautiful ironwork near the bay windows and the entrance door.

At the top of the façade, a bas-relief represents a basket with fruit falling out of it, which is strewn across the façade.

The house has retained its original floor plan. A central staircase, which has plenty of light because of the skylight above it, gives access to the rooms at the front and the back of the house. The kitchen is still in the cellar. On the ground floor, there is a study at the front of the house, while the dining room is at the back.

The sitting room can be found on the first floor, behind the loggia, which offers stunning views of Forest Park. Originally the view was designed to be even more expansive.

This house is comparable to Gustave Strauven's Saint-Cyr house, which he built in 1900 (see p. 79), because of its narrow façade and its impressive horseshoe-shaped arch.

In 1906, Arthur Nelissen built a striking home and studio for a manufacturer of enamelled plaques called Victor Delplanque, in Anderlecht at no. 162–164 Rue Georges Moreau. This was the first time he used decorative enamelled plaques on a façade, and over time this became one of his specialisations. The façade at 4, Avenue du Mont Kemmel, which was built in 1905, features such plaques.

At 6, Avenue du Mont Kemmel (unknown architect, 1905), the white lacquered brick façade features ceramic decorations on the sills and lintels of the window. These were produced in the factory of Célestin Helman, in Berchem-Sainte-Agathe. They are decorated with plant-based motifs, mainly poppies in white and orange against a turquoise backdrop.

Villa Beau-Site ▸

ANNO
1905

THIRD WALK

THE HEART OF SAINT-GILLES
FROM PLACE ANTOINE DELPORTE TO RUE VANDERSCHRICK

This walk takes on a tour of the neighbourhoods in the centre of Saint-Gilles. Like many of the other municipalities in the first tier, this commune experienced a real demographic revolution around the turn of the nineteenth and twentieth century. New neighbourhoods were developed for the lower and middle class, as well as retail and leisure facilities. During this visit we will also take a closer look at the Ægidium festival hall, which is currently being restored!

◀ House of the architect Georges Delcoigne, Place Morichar 14, 1899

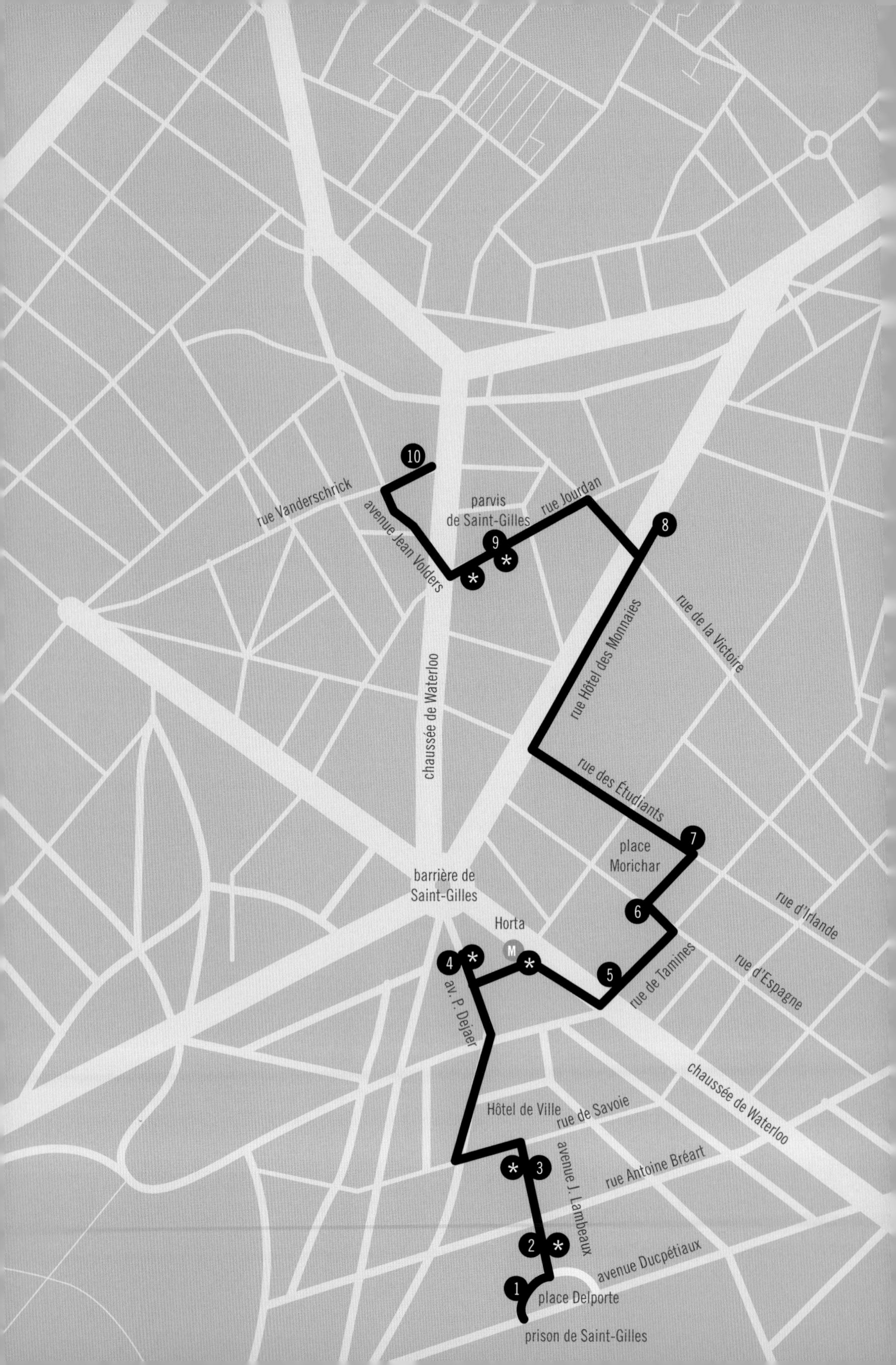

10
rue Vanderschrick
avenue Jean Volders
parvis
de Saint-Gilles
9
rue Jourdan
8
rue Hôtel des Monnaies
rue de la Victoire
chaussée de Waterloo
rue des Étudiants
7
place
Morichar
barrière de
Saint-Gilles
6
rue d'Irlande
Horta
M
4
5
rue de Tamines
rue d'Espagne
av. P. Dejaer
chaussée de Waterloo
Hôtel de Ville
rue de Savoie
avenue J. Lambeaux
3
rue Antoine Bréart
2
avenue Ducpétiaux
1
place Delporte
prison de Saint-Gilles

01 **HOUSE**
PLACE ANTOINE DELPORTE 17, 1060 SAINT-GILLES

02 **HOUSE AND OFFICE OF THE ARCHITECT PAUL HAMESSE**
AVENUE JEF LAMBEAUX 25, 1060 SAINT-GILLES

03 **PEEREBOOM HOUSE**
AVENUE JEF LAMBEAUX 12, 1060 SAINT-GILLES

04 **DE BECK HOUSE**
AVENUE PAUL DEJAER 9, 1060 SAINT-GILLES

05 **GROUP OF SIX HOUSES**
CHAUSSÉE DE WATERLOO 246-256, 1060 SAINT-GILLES

06 **VAN BELLINGHEN-TOMBERG HOUSE**
PLACE MORICHAR 41, 1060 SAINT-GILLES

07 **HOUSE OF THE ARCHITECT GEORGES DELCOIGNE**
PLACE MORICHAR 14, 1060 SAINT-GILLES

08 **HÔTEL WINSSINGER**
RUE DE L'HÔTEL DES MONNAIES 66, 1060 SAINT-GILLES

09 **ÆGIDIUM**
PARVIS DE SAINT-GILLES 18, 1060 SAINT-GILLES

10 **GROUP OF FOURTEEN HOUSES**
RUE VANDERSCHRICK 1-25, AVENUE JEAN VOLDERS 42-48 AND CHAUSSÉE DE WATERLOO 13-15, 1060 SAINT-GILLES

1/ HOUSE

Place Antoine Delporte 17, 1060 Saint-Gilles
Architect: Paul Hamesse
1907
Listed: 12 February 1998

The southern part of the commune of Saint-Gilles, which was built from 1892 onwards, extends from the large neo-medieval prison complex of Saint-Gilles (Joseph Jonas Dumont and François Derre. It is dominated by the commune's majestic town hall, which was built in the French neo-Renaissance style and inaugurated in 1904 (Albert Dumont).

No. 17 in Place Delporte is a typical example of Paul Hamesse's geometric Art Nouveau style. The plastered and painted façade, which rests on a blue stone and sandstone base, is subdivided into two staggered spans, one of which is set back. The entrance span, on the left, which is topped with pinnacles in carved stone, has a series of bay windows in various shapes. There is a basket-handle arch over the front door while the first-floor window is horseshoe-shaped. The second-floor window is T-shaped and the tiny window on the last floor has a hexagonal shape. The windowsills all feature a carved 'lip'. The same motif is repeated at the top of the span.

The house still has its original window frames and very geometric ironwork. The handle of the entrance door, combined with the slot of the letterbox, is typical of the architect's work.

Many of the original features of the house's interior, with adjoining three rooms, have been retained.

At 36 Avenue Jef Lambeaux, an eclectic house (Alfred Malchair, 1900) stands out because of the magnificent stained glass window above the entrance door, representing a flying goose, and the beautifully restored sgraffiti in which you can make out a woman's profile and a vagabond wandering through a landscape.

2/ HOUSE AND OFFICE OF THE ARCHITECT PAUL HAMESSE

Avenue Jef Lambeaux 25, 1060 Saint-Gilles
Architect: Paul Hamesse
1909-1910
Listed: 23 October 1997

Paul Hamesse and his brothers Georges and Léon worked in this corner house, which was built in 1909–1910, as attested by the plaque to the right of the entrance door.

This project, which is less austere than the house in Place Delporte, features many decorative elements, such as geometric garlands and egg-and-dart friezes. Its composition, its vertically elongated windows and its semi-circular gabled roof also point to the influence of the Viennese Secession, more in particular to one of its more illustrious representatives, Josef Olbrich (1867–1908), who combined modernity with historicist styles.

While the façades are different, they are built in the same white stone and faux stone, which rests on a base of pink sandstone rubble and blue stone. They are topped with a grooved frieze, which is interrupted by small serrated tablets, which have been decorated with an oval motif, which was originally gilded.

The façade in Avenue Lambeaux has only one span, the entrance. The bay windows are narrow and vertically elongated, with a semi-circular arch. On the upper floor, a cartouche with a date 'MXMX' refers to the date of construction (1910). The span on the bias connects the two façades. Each floor is different: the corner becomes a right angle on the ground floor, has a rounded oriel on the first and second floors while a small terrace sits in front of the imposing dormer, which resembles a turret on the uppermost floor.

The façade in Rue Antoine Bréart has rectangular bay windows, which have been decorated on the first floor with garlands of stylised flowers. An impressive gable, with a half-moon window and a frieze of ovals, caps the façade. The two latter spans do not extend beyond the ground floor.

The architect's descendants still live in the house, which has retained many of its original features, including the fixed furniture, the stained glass windows, the copper inlays, the stencilled paintings and the decorative scheme with stylised roses.

Paul Hamesse (1877–1956) was the son of a painter who studied architecture at the Academy of Fine Arts of Brussels where his brothers Georges (1873–1854) and Léon (1883–1958) studied painting. Paul Hamesse then trained with Paul Hankar and Alban Chambon, two architects with very different approaches, thanks to whom his career evolved into almost opposite directions. From Paul Hankar he retained the sense of geometric simplicity and a progressive view, which influenced him at the start of his career, from 1898 onwards. Alban Chambon, who designed theatres and hotels, taught him to use an eclectic vocabulary, which he used once he himself was tasked with the design of theatres and music halls.

In the early years of his career, the architect built buildings that were influenced by avant-garde movements such as the Viennese Secession, the Glasgow School of Art, English cottages, and so on. Paul Hamesse also specialised in adapting older buildings to newer tastes (Hôtel Cohn-Donnay, 1904). From 1908, he joined forces with his brothers, building cinemas and music halls in a more eclectic style, influenced by the late Secession. The Pathe company commissioned several cinemas from them in Belgium, including their Brussels cinema (1913).

After World War I and until the beginning of World War II, Paul Hamesse and his brothers also built several individual dwellings, apartment buildings and storefronts in the Art Deco style.

3/ HOUSE PEEREBOOM

Avenue Jef Lambeaux 12, 1060 Saint-Gilles
Architect: Georges Peereboom
1898
Listed: 6 July 2006

Georges Peereboom's father, who was also an architect but more importantly a municipal councillor in Saint-Gilles, commissioned this house from his son, who made a concerted effort to ensure it would be beautiful! Not much is known about Georges Peereboom (who died in 1930), as his archives were destroyed. He mainly worked in Saint-Gilles and his style veers between eclecticism and Art Nouveau. He also built a house in Place Jean Jacobs (see p. 147).

The white and blue stone façade stands out because of the shape of its bay windows and its window frames, which are different on every floor. As is often the case during the Art Nouveau period, the windows have small divisions. The oak entrance door features carved plant ornaments, and a small stained glass window as well as a small peephole. The handle also serves as the opening of the letterbox (the other letterboxes were added later).

The bay windows on the upper floor are topped with a plant-shaped stone stringcourse. Above the entrance door and its upper light, the stringcourse features a tympanum, decorated with an embossed pattern of flowers and foliage.

The top part of the façade, under the cornice, which is called entablature, is decorated by a frieze, which is punctuated by the cornice's modillions.

The house has pretty wrought iron balconies, which are more expressive on the ground floor, where the architect incorporated three-dimensional flowers in his design.

The rather eclectic interior has retained many of its original period elements. The house has been subdivided into apartments.

The two adjoining houses, at nos. 8 and 10 of Avenue Lambeaux, were also built by Georges Peereboom (1908). While no. 10 has a more neo-classical feel to it, no. 8 has some exceptional window frames, although they are more geometric in style than those of the architect's own house. The red brick façade features a stylised white brick decoration scheme in the entablature.

At 11, Avenue Lambeaux, the Art Nouveau house by Alphonse and Victor Boelens (1900) features a light brick façade combined with carved white stone elements. The house's original window frames, pretty oak entrance door, and ironwork in the shape of stylised insects have all been retained. The stone arches around the windows are particularly expressive. The entablature, which is punctuated by the modillions that support the cornice, is decorated with ceramic tiles.

The Peereboom house ▸

4/ DE BECK HOUSE

Avenue Paul Dejaer 9, 1060 Saint-Gilles
Architect: Gustave Strauven
1902
Listed: 13 July 2006

Finding a design by Gustave Strauven at this end of Brussels is rather unusual, as the prolific architect preferred to work in Schaerbeek and the squares neighbourhood.

The house, which was commissioned by a Mr De Beck, which has a shop on the ground floor, is typical of the architect's exuberant output. The building's verticality is underscored by the lot's narrow dimensions (it is only six metres wide) and by the top of the building, a gabled dormer with two decorative elements that are connected by ironwork.

The façade features a subtle combination of white and red bricks, with blue and white stone.

As the elevation increases, the width of the white and red bricks is reversed. The window frames, which are different on every floor, enhance the rhythm of the façade's composition.

The third and fourth floor have a trapezoidal oriel and balconies that are connected by ironwork railings and a metal column. There is a terrace above the oriel, with another balcony on top of it, which supported by two stone consoles.

On the opposite side of the street, at no. 10 Avenue Dejaer, the storefront and sgraffiti of the former Forge house and shop (Paul Hankar, 1898) are no longer there, but the wrought iron railings with geometric motifs (which were listed on 28 June 2001) are still in place.

Walk up Avenue Paul Dejaer to enter the small park, between no. 26 and no. 28, which will bring you to the entrance of the Horta pre-metro station. In the station, you can see an artwork titled 'Homage to Victor Horta', from 1993 by the architect Jean-Pierre Hoa. He has incorporated balustrades and stained glass windows of the Maison du Peuple (1895) and Hôtel Aubecq (1899), by Horta, which were demolished in spite of numerous protests. Hôtel Aubecq, on Avenue Louise, near La Cambre forest, was demolished in 1950, despite the intervention of Julia Carlsson, Horta's second wife, and Jean Delhaye, who admired Horta's work. They received a grant, however, for the dismantlement and conservation of part of the façade. In 2010, after being moved several times, the façade was finally reassembled on the floor of a warehouse in Schaerbeek, where it still awaits a decision about its future!

5/ GROUP OF SIX HOUSES

Chaussée de Waterloo 246-256, 1060 Saint-Gilles
Architect: Jean-Pierre Van Oostveen
1901
Listed: 8 May 2008

▲ Chaussée de Waterloo 254

At first glance, people are inclined not to pay much attention to this group of houses, although it deserves more even though some of the houses have been strongly altered. These six houses in the geometric Art Nouveau style were built for the same client, the widow Hellinckx. Not much is known about their architect, Jean-Pierre Van Oostveen (1873–1903), who did not build that many houses in Brussels. According to Françoise Aubry, the curator of the Horta Museum, these houses 'obviously are consistent with Paul Hankar's architectural approach. Their style is also very similar to that of Paul Hamesse. Curiously enough, there is such a formal kinship with his work here, that one might be inclined to say that Van Oosteveen and Hamesse worked together, perhaps in Hankar's studio. The windowsills are accentuated in the same way, the punctuation of the brick frames around the windows with hewn stone, and the stylised insect motifs of the ironwork ...'.[1]

Although their floor plans are identical, and are repeated three times, mirroring each other, the façade of each of the houses is different. The bay windows have different shapes, often with windowsills with a lip. The design of the window frames is original, with transoms with stained glass windows featuring geometric motifs, which are paired with wrought ironwork railings. A large part of the original woodwork – doors, window frames, bay window – has been replaced. The floor plan of the houses is very traditional, with three adjoining rooms and a lateral staircase. Except for the house at no. 254, all the ground-floor levels have been altered to accommodate a garage or a shop. The façade of no. 248 underwent the most radical transformation. Only the interiors of nos. 252 and 254 retained their original character.

6/ VAN BELLINGHEN-TOMBERG HOUSE

Place Morichar 41, 1060 Saint-Gilles
Architect: Ernest Blerot
1900
Listed: 6 July 2006

Place Louis Morichar was named after an alderman for public education and fine arts, and was built in 1898 on a former market garden.

The house was built for Mr Van Bellinghen-Tomberg, who was a trader of building materials and patented roofing slates. His warehouse occupied the adjoining lot (no. 42–44), as is evidenced from the sign in mauve and gold mosaic.

Ernest Blerot designed many houses, sometimes even in series, using the same vocabulary to build façades that always looked different. The composition of this façade heralds that of no. 15 Rue Darwin and no. 120 Avenue Brugmann (see p. 41). The difference lies in the decorative details however.

The façade is built in white stone from Euville, which has been remarkably well preserved, and has a trapezoidal bay window on the first floor, which is slightly off-centre to the right. It rests on a carved base, in the shape of an anemone, surrounded by foliage. The support of the bay window extends to the left, into a balcony with a wrought iron railing with organic shapes.

The windows are surmounted by tympani, that are wider on the first floor, and narrower on the second floor, and which feature mosaics. This is rather unique compared with the rest of Blerot's output, for which he tended to use sgraffito. The decoration of the large tympanum illustrates the start and end of the day, with a cockerel crowing at dawn to the left and an owl, the moon, and a tombstone to the right. The tympanum on the second floor features a group of swifts. The woodwork, window frames, and entrance door are all original. On the upper floor, the transoms are more geometric, while the large window on the first floor and the upper light with transom over the entrance door feature stained glass windows representing herons.

7/ HOUSE OF THE ARCHITECT GEORGES DELCOIGNE

Place Morichar 14, 1060 Saint-Gilles
Architect: Georges Delcoigne
1899
Listed: 6 July 2006

This perfectly preserved house is one of the rare Art Nouveau designs of the architect and entrepreneur Georges Delcoigne (1870–1916), whose output for the most part is neoclassical and eclectic in style.

The façade, which is made of white stone from Euville, has two asymmetrical and staggered spans, with a slightly protruding entrance span. The design is beautifully vertical, which is enhanced by the narrowness of the bay windows and the stone mullions that separate them and which run from floor to floor, visually extending the house. The main span, on each floor, is subdivided into three narrow windows: with two mullions on the ground floor, referring to neo-Gothic architecture, and a triple window on the upper floors. The entrance is subdivided into narrow windows on each floor. The first two have been covered with oak panels and small lights with transoms.

Every element of the façade refers to organic, plant shapes from the consoles and the mullions to the railings and the ironwork. The sills of the second-floor windows have been decorated with panels with sgraffiti with a highly stylised vegetal decoration, in which two allegorical female figures are visible. The one on the left evokes music and singing (one can make out a lyre, a pan flute, a trumpet and a singing face), while the figure on the right represents painting and architecture (it features a painter's palette and brushes as well as a mallet). A five-pointed star in each of the panels might be a discreet reference to Freemasonry. The Masons consider the five-pointed star a reference to illumination. However, this remains to be proven. The façade also features beautiful ironwork on some of the windows and balconies. Finally, all the woodwork is still the original woodwork.

The entrance is especially refined. The elegant design of the entrance door, with its copper letterbox, is combined with a narrow window, under one and the same arch. A rather unusual wrought iron scraper has been installed under the window.

The floor plan is traditional, with adjoining rooms and its mix of styles reflects the tastes of the upper middle classes of the Belle Epoque.

The Flemish neo-Renaissance style is combined here with Art Nouveau elements.

8/ HÔTEL WINSSINGER

Rue de l'Hôtel des Monnaies 66, 1060 Saint-Gilles
Architect: Victor Horta
1894-1897
Listed: 7 December 1984

In 1894, Camille Winssinger, a close associate of Ernest Solvay, asked Victor Horta to build him a home. The architect would go on to write in his *Mémoires*[2] that the mansion's size was disproportionate in respect to the neighbourhood, which was deemed unpopular. He also stipulated that the floor plan was influenced to a great extent by the fact that Winssinger's wife was sick and needed peace and rest. At the same time, Winssinger also needed the space to host business receptions. The upper floor is occupied by the reception areas, a large vestibule, a sitting room, and a small and a large dining room, while the parents sleep on the upper floor. The mezzanine has a billiard room.
From the start, Winssinger, 'who was an engineer and who was as precise as a chronometer and as sharp as a blade from Toledo[3]' expressed his concerns about the architect, whom he felt was too young, even though he admired Horta's Hôtel Tassel, which he had just completed. He feared that he would be unable to overcome the instability of the land. Once the foundation had been completed, the project was able to continue without a hitch. After Winssinger died in 1924, his heirs asked Horta to transform the mansion into an apartment building. He added one floor. The main stairwell, which is visible in the slightly protruding third span of the façade because of the divisions that refer to the various landings, is interrupted on the upper floor. The stairwell of the service stairs was remodelled to add a lift to the upper floor apartments. The stained glass windows and murals with their plant motifs in the main stairwell disappeared around this time. In 1946, the architect Henri Jacobs (Jr) undertook a new round of alterations, when the insurance company Le Lion Belge moved into the ground floor and mezzanine. The carriage gate was covered and a large annex with offices built in part of the garden.
In 2004, Michel Gilbert, a real estate broker who is passionate about Horta's work and who already owns several other buildings by the architect, bought the building. It was subsequently restored by Barbara Van der Wee. The winter garden and the stairwell to the first floor were restored. To date, the building is still used as office premises and rental apartments.

The white stone façade, which is highlighted with blue stone, looks livelier thanks to the projection of the third span, thus breaking with the overall classicism of the composition. The carriage entrance is slightly off centre. On the first floor, the large window of the bow window is punctuated by four small cast iron columns that extent to the railing of the terrace above it. The bow window is flanked by two balconies with elegant wrought iron railings, supported by elegant curved consoles. The large windows on the ground floor and first floor are accentuated by the typical organic stone Art Nouveau mouldings that Horta used so often.
Despite undergoing various transformations, much of the interior, which Horta drew down to the smallest detail, including the furniture, has been retained or restored: mosaic floors, a marble staircase, an exposed metal structure, cast iron, door handles with a tortious design, sconces, vegetal ceiling mouldings, and so on.

9/ ÆGIDIUM

Parvis de Saint-Gilles 18, 1060 Saint-Gilles
Architect: Guillaume Segers
1905
Listed: 8 June 2006

The Parvis Saint-Gilles is located in the historic core of the municipality, which developed around the first Church of Saint-Gilles. From 1862 until 1878, the population grew significantly prompting the construction of a larger church along Chaussée de Waterloo (Victor Besme). In 1900, the authorities ordered the construction of the current Parvis, in the interest of embellishing and upgrading the locality. It is still used as a marketplace today. Its elongated curved shape is lined with apartment buildings and stores that were built in the early twentieth century.

The Ægidium, which was built in 1905, was initially called Diamant-Palace and later Panthéon-Palace. The edifice was sold in 1929 to a canon, who transformed it into a Catholic charity. It was renamed Ægidium in the Thirties, a direct reference to the parish as Ægidius is the Latin form of Gilles or Giles.

The façade was built in a neo-classical eclectic style and does not in any way reflect the exuberance of the building's interior. There is an inscription 'Ægidium' over the top of the entrance to the right. Originally there was a café on the ground floor, with a monumental staircase with two flights of stairs leading up to the meeting room on the upper floor, with its lavish Louis XV decoration and a large events hall with a Moorish design scheme. Soon, the Ægidium became a popular place with the upper middle classes, as there was nothing like it elsewhere in Brussels. In 1933, the café was redecorated in the modernist style by the architect Léon Denis while the events hall was transformed into a cinema with a new projection booth. In 1956, the ceiling of the Louis XV room was replaced with a concrete slab. The building, which had become outdated, was finally vacated in 1985.

Despite all the alterations, the Ægidium has retained much of its original charm and was listed because of the 'exceptionally rich decorative repertoire[4]'. The 4,700 sq. m. space will hopefully be renovated and given a new designation in line with its architecture and history.

Many of the building's interior decorations are clearly inspired by Art Nouveau. The ground floor cloakroom has Art Nouveau wainscoting, and ceramic tiles featuring bucolic scenes, by Helman. The stairwell, which has a skylight, is designed in the Beaux-Arts style with Art Nouveau elements. The walls have been decorated with mirrors, which visually multiply the spaces.

The Moorish-style room is unique in Belgium. It has a small stage at one end and a gallery at mid height. Above the stage, a crucifix, which is somewhat

▾ Cage d'escalier de l'Ægidium

swallowed up by the rest of the design scheme, refers to the Ægidium's last use. The lavish decoration, combining wood panelling and stucco work, draws on Moorish architecture, albeit with a lot of fantasy, combining arches and arcatures with multiple lobes or Moorish arches with monumental divided consoles, columns, and pillars painted in faux marble with gilded capitals, mirrors, and rosettes. The coffered ceiling of the room was lit up by thousands of light bulbs that were reflected in the mirrors in the panelling. The whole effect must have been absolutely enchanting!

At 37–39, Parvis de Saint-Gilles, Alfred Malchair built a Maison du Peuple in 1905 for the Société Coopérative de Bruxelles. This was a meeting place for political debate and for culture. In 1914, Lenin gave a speech here. In the Sixties, the Maison du Peuple finally closed and the building was used for various purposes before being acquired by the municipality. It was restored from 1997 until 2002. The Flemish neo-Renaissance building has been extended at the rear with a large hall, with an exposed Art Nouveau-style metal structure.

At 19, Parvis de Saint-Gilles, the office of the Christian Health Insurance Fund still has two ceramic panels, by Helman, featuring bucolic scenes. They were originally produced for the Grande Triperie Saint-Gilloise (a tripe manufacturer), which was located here from 1936 until 1993 (listed on 8 December 2005).

10/ GROUP OF FOURTEEN HOUSES

Rue Vanderschrick 1-25, Avenue Jean Volders 42-48 and Chaussée de Waterloo 13–15, 1060 Saint-Gilles
Architect: Ernest Blerot
1900-1902
Listed: 8 August 1988

Saint-Gilles has a unique group of buildings. This group of fourteen houses by the architect Ernast Blerot extends along the entire uneven numbered side of Rue Vanderschrick, from Chaussée de Waterloo to Avenue Volders.

Once again, Blerot demonstrated his knack for creating individual buildings with very similar plans. Small buildings with large storefronts coexist harmoniously with residential buildings. Most of the buildings feature the architect's signature and a date. Some are built in light brick, others in white stone, and all have a blue stone base. The bases are all slightly flared. The façades look livelier because of the bay windows, there are upper lights with stained glass windows above the entrance doors, and the windows are often grouped under large stone arches, with an organic shape, featuring sgraffiti. The transoms, which are all original, often have stained glass windows with floral motifs. The wrought iron railings of the balconies are of exceptional quality. The wood cornices rest on slender, ornate modillions. Finally, the façades are often capped with a gabled dormer, which in some cases is triangular, and is typical of Blerot's architectural style.

The group of buildings was completed in two phases for the widow Elsom, an annuitant. The buildings in Chaussée de Waterloo and no. 1 through 13 in Rue Vanderschrick were built in 1900. No. 15 through 25 in Rue Vanderschrick and the buildings in Rue Jean Volders were completed in 1902.

In 1911, Emma Elsom, the widow's daughter, built an events hall in the courtyard, called the Regina Palace, which could be accessed from no. 13 Chaussée de Waterloo and through the carriage gate at no. 7–9 of Rue Vanderschrick. It was enlarged in 1913, and razed to the ground following a fire in 1974, after which was transformed into a warehouse. It is currently used as a playground.

After analysing the almanacs of 1914[5], we established that the storefronts were occupied by a supplier to seamstresses and milliners, an ice-cream shop, and a café. The homes and apartments were occupied by several sales representatives, some annuitants, a civil servant, and an electrician, all members of the middle class!

Some of these houses were restored. In the early noughties, Martin Gray (1922–2016) acquired the houses at nos. 3-5-7 and 9 of Rue Vanderschrick and no. 13 in Chaussée de Waterloo after permanently relocating to Belgium. He undertook the restoration of his properties. The French-American writer, of Polish origin, became famous after the publication of his book 'Au Nom de Tous les Miens' (1971), in which he describes the dramatic events, which caused him to lose his family twice, first because of the Nazis and then because of the fire in his house in the south of France. After the war, he moved to the United States, and started importing Art Nouveau furniture and objects to resell them to American customers. The restoration of these houses are his tribute to Brussels Art Nouveau. Furthermore, Gray became particularly enamoured with the neighbourhood: 'I am Jewish, Polish, America, French, and Belgian, which is why I like this multicultural place so much. I feel a kind of artistic impetus here. Saint-Gilles is like the Greenwich Village of Brussels, in a sense'.[6] You can end your work by stopping at La Porteuse d'Eau, on the corner of Jean Volders and Rue Vanderschrick. But don't be fooled: its Art Nouveau interior dates from ... 1988!

▲ Corner of Rue Vanderschrick and Avenue Jean Volders

The name of **Ernest Blerot (1870–1957)** is inextricably linked with Art Nouveau as a style. This architect, who studied at Saint-Luc in Schaerbeek, is part of the second generation of Art Nouveau architects, who ensured that the middle class could afford this style.

From 1897 onwards, when he established his own architect's practice, Blerot built about seventy homes and residential buildings, often in series, working as a real estate developer and contractor. He preferred to work in Ixelles, Saint-Gilles, and Forest. He usually stuck to the traditional floor plan of Brussels houses, but succeeded in giving each of his buildings an individual identity, while often using a very similar decorative vernacular.

After World War I, Blerot rebuilt the family castle of Elzenwalle, in Vormezele near Ypres, which was destroyed during the war. The result is an original building, in reinforced concrete, with Art Nouveau references.

FOURTH WALK

CINQUANTENAIRE AND THE SQUARES NEIGHBOURHOOD
FROM MAISON CAUCHIE TO SQUARE GUTENBERG

A trail through one of Brussels' most prestigious neighbourhoods, starting at the Cauchie house, which has been given a new lease of life by the Dessicy family. After walking through the Cinquantenaire park, the trail takes you to the squares where you will find some of the most iconic Art Nouveau buildings in Brussels, including Saint Cyr house by Gustave Strauven and Hôtel van Eetvelde, one of Victor Horta's works which is listed as UNESCO World Heritage.

◂ Saint Cyr house, Square Ambiorix 11, Gustave Strauven, 1900

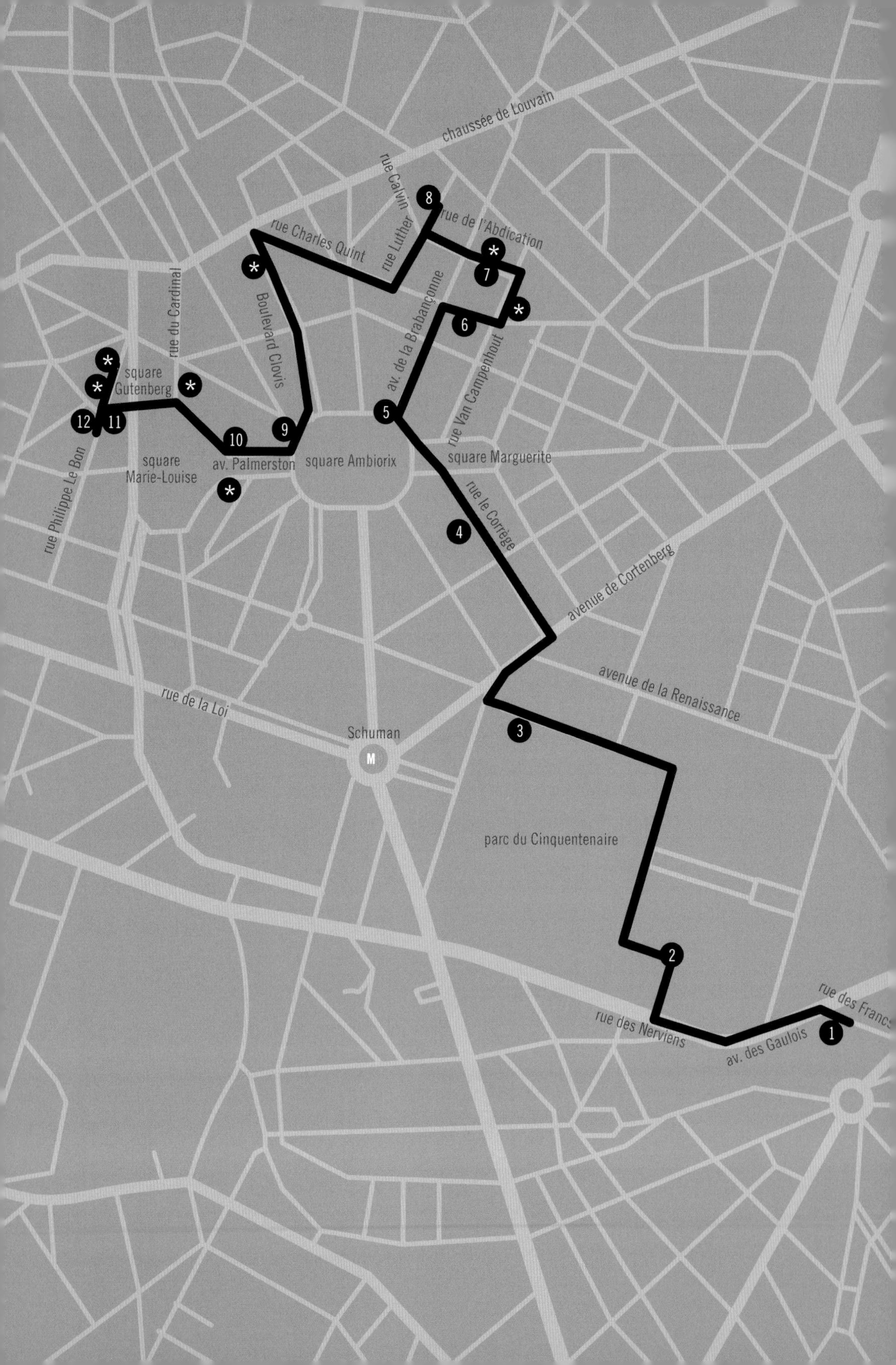

chaussée de Louvain
rue Calvin
rue de l'Abdication
rue Charles Quint
rue Luther
av. de la Brabançonne
Boulevard Clovis
rue du Cardinal
square Gutenberg
rue Van Campenhout
square Marie-Louise
av. Palmerston
square Ambiorix
square Marguerite
rue Philippe Le Bon
rue le Corrège
avenue de Cortenberg
avenue de la Renaissance
rue de la Loi
Schuman
M
parc du Cinquentenaire
rue des Nerviens
av. des Gaulois
rue des Francs
1
2
3
4
5
6
7
8
9
10
11
12

01 **HOUSE AND STUDIO OF THE ARCHITECT PAUL CAUCHIE**
RUE DES FRANCS 5, 1040 ETTERBEEK

02 **ART NOUVEAU COLLECTION OF THE CINQUANTENAIRE MUSEUM**
PARC DU CINQUANTENAIRE 10, 1000 BRUSSELS

03 **PAVILION OF THE HUMAN PASSIONS**
PARC DU CINQUANTENAIRE, 1000 BRUSSELS

04 **HOUSE OF THE ARCHITECT ÉDOUARD RAMAEKERS**
RUE LE CORRÈGE 35, 1000 BRUSSELS

05 **SAINT CYR HOUSE**
SQUARE AMBIORIX 11, 1000 BRUSSELS

06 **HOUSE AND STUDIO OF THE PAINTER ARTHUR ROGIERS**
RUE CHARLES-QUINT 103, 1000 BRUSSELS

07 **HOUSE OF THE SCULPTOR PIERRE BRAECKE**
RUE DE L'ABDICATION 31, 1000 BRUSSELS

08 **HOUSE OF THE ARCHITECT GUSTAVE STRAUVEN**
RUE LUTHER 28 / RUE CALVIN 5, 1000 BRUSSELS

09 **QUAKER HOUSE**
SQUARE AMBIORIX 50, 1000 BRUSSELS

10 **HÔTEL VAN EETVELDE AND APARTMENT BUILDING**
AVENUE PALMERSTON 2-4, 1000 BRUSSELS

11 **HOUSES**
SQUARE GUTENBERG 5 ET RUE PHILIPPE LE BON 55, 1000 BRUSSELS

12 **HOUSE OF THE ARCHITECT VICTOR TAELEMANS**
RUE PHILIPPE LE BON 70, 1000 BRUSSELS

1/ HOUSE AND STUDIO OF THE ARCHITECT PAUL CAUCHIE

RUE DES FRANCS 5, 1040 ETTERBEEK

Architect: Paul Cauchie
1904-1905
Listed: 16 March 1995

The painter, graphic designer, furniture designer and architect Paul Cauchie (1875–1952) highlighted the various aspects of the decorative renewal that is so characteristic of Art Nouveau in his work. He is one of the main representatives of the sgraffito technique, which was very popular at the turn of the twentieth century.

Shortly before his marriage to Caroline—better known as Lina—Voet, whom he met at the Academy of Fine Arts Brussels, Cauchie started work on what was to become their house. It is one of the most original Art Nouveau works in Brussels, influenced both by the Glasgow-based architect Charles Rennie Mackintosh (1868–1928) and the Viennese Secession. Paul Cauchie developed the theme of the poster-façade by covering it almost entirely with a vast composition of sgraffiti.

The façade's composition is symmetrical. On the street level, a porch that has been incorporated into the building, with wood pillars in front of it, serves as the entrance to the basement and upper floor. On either side of the porch, two sgraffiti panels provide information about the many disciplines practiced by the owner of the house. They include decoration, private art classes, painting, redesigns of interiors and façades, sgraffiti, furniture, and so on. On the upper floor, a balcony with an iron railing with a very geometric design has been installed in front of a panel in the centre of the façade, with a sgraffito representing a female figure, who faces us. The inscription reads 'PAR NOUS/POUR NOUS'. Finally, on the uppermost floor, which is also the floor of the studio, a large circular window, with a balcony, protrudes from the monumental sgraffito featuring eight female figures, the allegories of the arts: the figures at the top embody painting (palette and brushes) and music (lyre). The three figures below them, on the left, are associated with sculpture (compass, figurine, hammer, and chisel), the three figures on the right evoke architecture (temple) and silversmithing (necklace), while the attributes of the last allegorical figure cannot be identified. The very slender muses, which are represented in profile, with their undulating tresses, are all covered in veils that have been draped around their sinuous bodies. The backdrop is dotted with highly

stylised roses, which Cauchie often uses in his sgraffiti and which look very similar to the diaphragm of a camera.
The overhanging cornice is surmounted by a railing, flanked by huge stone cubes that vertically extend the façade.
The façade has a rough and smooth coating. The materials underneath are not that visible. The façade's design, which consists of circular and square shapes, is very elaborate. Here straight lines reign supreme, which is very unusual as the Art Nouveau style was dominated by curved lines until then.
The architect also designed the house's furniture. The walls of the upper floor are decorated with panels with sgraffiti, representing the allegories of the arts, echoing the façade.
Paul and Line Cauchie lived in this house until they died in 1952 and 1969 respectively. In 1971, their daughter applied for planning permission to demolish the house and build an apartment building instead. The neighbourhood residents and various official associations voiced their dissent and the planning permit was denied.
The house was listed in 1975 but continued to decline. In 1980, Guy and Léo Dessicy finally bought the house and undertook its restoration. The entire process would take fifteen years. The restoration of the sgraffiti, at a time when artisans were no longer familiar with the technique, is considered exemplary, because of the restorer's cautious and successful approach. Since 1994, the main rooms and the basement, which is now a gallery, are open to the public. The upper floors are rented out. The daughters and granddaughters of Guy and Léo Dessicy are now in charge of the continuation of this amazing adventure, welcoming visitors to the house.

The term **'sgraffito'** is derived from the Italian word *graffiare,* which means 'to scratch'. This wall decoration technique consists of covering a surface with dark mortar, either dark red or black, followed by a fine layer of clear mortar. While the upper layer is still wet, the artist scratches the outline of a drawing into the mortar with a stylus, revealing the underlying, darker layer and creating a dark outline. The various planes can then be coloured. This technique, which was very popular during the Renaissance, was rediscovered at the end of the nineteenth century. It is often associated with Art Nouveau projects. The sgraffiti deteriorate because of the weather and pollution and if they are not maintained they may disappear. The technique was no longer practiced by the time the restoration of the Cauchie House started in the Eighties. This restoration was a first and the Royal Institute of Artistic Heritage (IRPA) assisted the restorers, Marc Henricot and Walter Schudel, with their arduous task. The sgraffiti were detached from the façade, fragment by fragment, with a scalpel. They were then restored and treated in the workshop, after which they were affixed to the façade again.
Nowadays, several restorers are trained to restore sgraffiti and restorations are now carried out on the spot.
Sgraffiti artists rarely sign their work. The names of the most important artists are known to us, however:

- **Adolphe Crespin** (1859–1944) often worked with Paul Hankar. His art is very similar to illustration and he especially liked to represent animals.
- **Privat Livemont** (1861–1936), who was influenced by symbolism, often worked with Henri Jacobs. The female figure played an important role in his work.
- **Paul Cauchie** (1875–1952) developed an original, rather geometric style of his own, which often featured women in profile, with flowers in their hair. His panels are dotted with constellations of stylised roses.
- **Gabriel Van Dievoet** (1875–1934) worked as a painter and decorator and excelled at representing stylised flowers.
- **Géo Ponchon** (1877–1959) often represented birds and foliage. He also offered a maintenance system to his clients.

A specialised association (called Groupe d'Études et de Recherches Peintures Murales – Sgraffites Culturels (GERPM-SC ASBL) studies these **sgraffiti**.

PORTRAIT: THE DESSICY FAMILY

Guy and Léo Dessicy, who own the Cauchie house since 1980, also had it restored and opened it to the public. Nowadays their daughters and grandchildren have taken over their life's work. We met the eldest daughter, Michèle Dessicy, at the Cauchie house for a chat.

Cécile Dubois: When your parents bought the house, it was in very bad shape. Didn't you wonder at the time what they were letting themselves in for?
Michèle Dessicy: Not at the time, no, because our parents had no intention at the time of opening the house to the public. They hoped to rent it out. I was thirty years old at the time. We were all asked to contribute, as well as our husbands and partners. Actually, none of us ever lived here even though at times it did feel like it. And yet, we all have plenty of memories that are related to the house. We meet here at Christmas and for birthdays. We gave this house a new lease on life. This house has several souls: that of the Cauchie family, that of our family, and that of the tenants, who in some cases became friends.

CD: What prompted the opening of the house to the public?
MD: In 1994, we organised an exhibition here of the paintings of Paul Cauchie and his wife Carolina. Soon after, we established a not-for-profit association, and we regularly opened the house to the public. My parents served as guides, and we, the daughter, took turns welcoming visitors and selling tickets. It all went very well. We all have good memories of those early days.

CD: But didn't your parents buy the house purely by chance?
MD: No, they came upon it one day during a walk and they fell in love with it on sight because it was a very special house. But it was not for sale! They obtained the address of the owner, Paul Cauchie's daughter. She was very happy to sell the house, which could not be demolished because it was a listed property. As such, she could not incorporate it in real estate project. My parents also bought paintings by Paul Cauchie from her.

CD: Were there any surprises during the restoration?
MD: My parents were happily surprised, seven years after they bought the house, to discover the sgraffiti in the dining room, which had been covered with wallpaper and newspapers. The sgraffiti had been preserved almost intact.

CD: Did your father have a special relationship with comic strip designers?
MD: My father was twelve years old when he made the acquaintance of Hergé, who hired him later on as a colourist. My father subsequently became the director of Publiart, the ad agency of Editions du Lombard where he worked with comic strip designers. Many of them became his friends. At the end of the Seventies, Hergé and my father thought about creating a Tintin Museum in the Cauchie House. Hergé was interested in it, and we even have a letter in which he expresses his enthusiasm. After Hergé died, they abandoned the project. My parents helped establish the Belgian Comic Strip Centre, which opened in 1989, in the former Waucquez department store, which Horta designed.

CD: So what is the status now and what are your intentions for the future?
MD: Our parents left us this magnificent gem, but it's a serious responsibility. We like meeting people, sharing, and learning from them. We cannot force the next generation to become involved in the project although I do hope that some of our children will continue this undertaking. I personally would prefer it if the house were managed by people who are passionate about it, who maintain the convivial, family aspect. At the same time, we need to be realistic. The idea is not to turn the house into a museum. The fact that part of the house is rented out, that it is not a museum, is what keeps it alive. On the financial level, we need this rent as we receive almost no government grants. People like to see that people really live here. We eat here, we have conversations, we laugh, we

organise small exhibitions, and we even made chocolate sgraffiti. I give writing workshops.[1] Artists exhibit their work here. These are all small-scale projects perhaps, but they draw visitors and are fun!

This interview took place in June 2016. Guy Dessicy passed away on 27 July 2016.

Léo and Guy Dessicy surrounded by their daughters: left to right, Pacou, Michèle, Claire, and Dominique. Gouache by Paul Cauchie, *Le Verger Blanchi*, 1924.

2/ ART NOUVEAU COLLECTION OF THE CINQUANTENAIRE MUSEUM

PARC DU CINQUANTENAIRE 10, 1000 BRUSSELS

The Wolfers department store gallery gives an overview of the main trends in the decorative arts from 1890 until 1940, and displays sculptures, glassware, ceramics, and silver. Masterpieces include a pair of candlesticks by Henry Van de Velde or chryselephantine sculptures that were created for the colonial exhibition in Tervuren in 1897. The display cases in which these items are exhibited were designed by Victor Horta for the Wolfers department store and were donated to the museum when the building was sold (see p. 162).
The restoration and opening, at the end of 2017, of the Wolfers department store is the first phase of a large-scale project. Several items of furniture, by Victor Horta and Léon Sneyers among others, are currently in storage. They will be integrated in the new display, scheduled for 2020.

▲ Charles Van der Stappen's *The Mysterious Sphinx*, 1897, ivory and silver

3/ PAVILION OF THE HUMAN PASSIONS
PARC DU CINQUANTENAIRE, 1000 BRUSSELS

Architect: Victor Horta
1890-1899
Listed: 18 November 1976

An air of scandal continues to surround this building, which remained closed to the public for a long time and was even somewhat abandoned. Some say that when it opened at the end of the nineteenth century, the upper middle classes were so shocked at the sight of the relief inside that a wall had to be built to conceal it from the gaze of the passers-by. But this is pure legend of course!

In 1889, Jef Lambeaux (1852–1908)—who was an Antwerp sculptor—presented his sketch for a relief, *Human Passions*[2] at the triennial Salon in Ghent. The work provoked quite a controversy and some critics felt that it lacked cohesion. Nonetheless, the state commissioned this work from the artist, to be executed in marble. The young Victor Horta received a simultaneous commission, through the intermediary of his teacher, the architect Alphonse Balat. It was his first large-scale project, and he was tasked to build a pavilion in the Cinquantenaire Park for this relief.

Horta designed a small, open neoclassical temple, with four columns on the façade. The relief was to be installed at the back of the building. Initially, the architect and the sculptor agreed on this design. Construction commenced in 1891. During the works, however, Lambeaux changed his mind and demanded that the building be closed so the relief would only be illuminated from above, by the light that came in through the skylight in the building's roof. Horta did not agree however and the building was completed as originally agreed. A few days after the inauguration, on 1 October 1899, a wooden partition was put up behind the columns, concealing the relief view and Horta was ordered to transform the building accordingly. He begrudgingly supplied new plans in 1906, which included the construction of a façade after moving the columns. Lambeaux did not live to see the final result, which was completed in 1910.

The pavilion, which is clad with white Euville and Savonnières stone, already heralds the Art Nouveau style. Although Horta used a relatively formal classical architectural style here, he already managed to incorporate some of the elements of the future style in his design. He prefered continuous lines, curved partitions, and softened angles. The lower part of the walls, which flares slightly, and the base with its curved profile make it look as if the building is rising up from the ground. The top of the columns is grooved, gently connecting the column shaft with the capital and its plant decoration.

The gentle curve of the pediment softens its lines.

Inside, the walls are clad with panels of yellow marble from Siena. The relief (12 metres long, 8 metres wide) was affixed to the wall at the back. Carved from seventeen blocks of white Carrara marble and it is illuminated by the light from the skylight. Its lavish composition of interlaced bodies illustrates the happiness and sins of humanity, with Christ and Death dominating the scene.

The pavilion was recently restored and is now open to the public again.

Pavilion of the Human Passions ▶
Detail from the relief, *Human Passions,* by Jef Lambeaux ▶

4/ HOUSE OF THE ARCHITECT ÉDOUARD RAMAEKERS

RUE LE CORRÈGE 35, 1000 BRUSSELS

Architect: Édouard Ramaekers
1899
Listed: 5 March 2007

Édouard Ramaekers (1864–1961) studied at the Ecole St. Luc in Schaerbeek and was famous for his neo-Gothic designs. He also built several buildings at the seaside and in the Congo.

For his own house, the architect chose to combine neo-Gothic architecture with Art Nouveau elements. This project is probably his best.

The façade's very slender structure corresponds with the proportions that are so typical of Gothic architecture. It is three times higher than its width and has an equilateral triangular gable.

The decorative scheme of the façade and the interior, which beautifully combines neo-Gothic elements with Art Nouveau, was very carefully thought out. It demonstrates Ramaekers's perfect mastery and craftsmanship—a tradition that was revived in the neo-Gothic style.

The façade has large, wide windows, which have been arranged in an original manner, and which show that the architect had fully grasped the principles of Art Nouveau. The façade looks very colourful because of the subtle combination of red and white bricks, and the colours of the sgraffiti and the stained glass windows. A wide bay window in wood rests on four consoles of Gothic inspiration on the upper floor. Sgraffiti have been added in between, representing a radiant sun flanked by two flying storks. The sills of the bay window are decorated with brick arches filled with sgraffiti with floral motifs. The window transoms echo the broken arches with their stained glass windows.

The dormer windows are joined under a semi-circular arch. The gable is punctuated by five white brick pilasters, which accentuate the building's verticality.

The ground floor is striking. The architect built a blue stone and pink rubble base. The ironwork on the cellar window is outstanding. Its organic curved lines follow the lines of the stained glass windows.

The top of the entrance door stands out because of the openwork. Here, ironwork and woodwork are combined to evoke a peacock's tail. The letterbox, the door handle, and the escutcheon of the lock and the knocker are real works of art.

The interior, with its adjoining rooms, is just as colourful as the façade. The floor of the entrance hall is covered with mosaics. The panelling in the hall and the stairwell is covered wits ceramic tiles, the doors all feature stained glass windows.

We now walk to the neighbourhood of the Squares, which was built in 1875 by the architect Gédéon Bordiau. It illustrates urban planning developments in Brussels at the end of the twentieth century. The neighbourhood, which is famous for its elegant town houses, in the eclectic style, however, is the best place in the city to see examples of the Brussels Art Nouveau style.

5/ SAINT CYR HOUSE

SQUARE AMBIORIX 11, 1000 BRUSSELS

Architect: Gustave Strauven
1900
Listed: 8 August 1988

This extraordinary house is probably the most photographed Art Nouveau house in Brussels! Built for the artist/painter and decorator Georges Léonard de Saint Cyr, it is built on a plot of land that is barely four metres wide, demonstrating the architect's ingenuity in the decoration of its façades. The house has one single span, with an unencumbered structure, and opens out onto the square on every floor with a wide and tall window. The shape and frame of each window is different. On either side of the single span, two brick and stone pilasters seem to support the ring on top of the façade. The entrance design is original to say the least. The staircase starts in the right half of the small front garden, leading up to a terrace to the left, in one single curve. The service entrance is concealed on the left, under the steps.

The platform's railing serves as a base for the two cast iron columns that support the first floor balcony's triangular slab. The railing of this balcony incorporates two columns that support the second floor balcony, which protrudes less. On the third floor, the brick ring is an artifice. It stands out from the façade, whereas the French window in front of it, which has the same shape, is connected to the roof. The ring therefore does not play a structural role but produces the extraordinary effect that has made this house so famous, even attracting international visitors. Finally, an impressive wrought iron crest surmounts this stunning design, like a masterful flourish.

The house has a small front garden/yard, which is bordered by a wrought iron fence with an exuberant design. To compensate for the narrowness of the parcel of land, the architect maximised the house's height and depth, to the garden's detriment. The rooms are arranged at the front and back of the house, on either side of the main stairwell, occupying the house's entire width. The stairwell is illuminated with plenty of light from above. The decoration is extremely diverse. The

dining room at the rear of the house, on the first floor, was designed in the Flemish neo-Renaissance style while the stairwell is in the neo-Empire style. There is a Chinese sitting room, dating from 1925, at the front of the house, on the first floor.
The façade was recently restored. Francis Metzger of the architect's firm Ma² is currently restoring the interior.

Gustave Strauven (1878–1919) trained at the Ecole Saint Luc in Schaerbeek and subsequently trained with Victor Horta at the time that he was building the Maison du Peuple and Hôtel van Eetvelde (1896–1897). He then spent one year working in Zurich, for a leading architect's firm before establishing his own architect's practice in 1899, at the age of 21 years. A real virtuoso, Strauven is part of the second generation of Art Nouveau architects, who followed in the footsteps of the pioneers while also making the style more affordable. His clients did not have the budget for a ashlar façade. But this did not bother him in the least. His extraordinary ingenuity enabled him to design façades with decorations that were inspired by nature, which are considered rather flamboyant today. Take a closer look, however, and you will soon realise that Strauven's design is very rational despite its exuberance. The architect also patented several inventions, including several new systems that he used in his buildings, as a well a monocycle, with a single wheel in which the cyclist placed him or herself to pedal the bike.
Gustave Strauven's work, which mainly consists of houses and apartment buildings, can be found in Brussels and Tournai for the most part.
He was drafted during World War I and died of tuberculosis in 1919.

6/ HOUSE-STUDIO OF THE PAINTER ARTHUR ROGIERS

RUE CHARLES-QUINT 103, 1000 BRUSSELS

Architect: Paul Hamesse
1898
Listed: 8 August 1988

The young Paul Hamesse established his own architect's practice when he built this house and studio for the painter and decorator Arthur Rogiers. At the time, he was still working for Paul Hankar. This design also shows the extent to which his master's geometric Art Nouveau style influenced his work.
The very pared down façade, which is almost industrial looking with its exposed metal lintels, combines red and white bricks with a wooden bay window and a small terrace. The architect's real challenge consisted in combining the house and studio in such a small surface area. The private apartment, on the upper floor, is very small. The large studio on the floor above it has been conceived as a duplex. A staircase offers access to an open gallery that extends across the main façade, and gives access to the small terrace. The studio has plenty of light, from the bay window, the large window and the skylight in the front part of the roof, which is invisible from the street level. The façade is refined in its detail. The entrance door and the cellar window are integrated in stone frames that have been carved in an original manner. The wooden door, with its sinuous design, is surmounted by a transom window with Japanese-style divisions and coloured glass. The metal opening of the letterbox is still visible to the right in the blue stone base.
The cellar window has bars in front of it, the lines of which spread out, recalling the feathers of a

▲ House and studio of the painter Arthur Rogiers

peacock's tail. The corners of the bay window, which are supported by two stone consoles, feature decorative profiles.
In 1902, the interior was slightly altered, probably by Paul Hamesse and again in 1908, at the request of the new owner, the writer Jules Potvin, who was also the librarian at the Royal Academy of Fine Arts.

At no. 51 in Rue Van Campenhout, Gustave Strauven's Kwachet house, which he built in 1901, immediately attracts the eye. The shape of the windows, the polychromy which he created by combining red and white bricks, the stained glass windows, and the blue stone elements. They are all typical of the architect's style, which is so often characterised by an abundant decoration (listed on 29 February 1984 and 2 July 1992).

7/ HOUSE OF THE SCULPTOR PIERRE BRAECKE

RUE DE L'ABDICATION 31, 1000 BRUSSELS

Architect: Victor Horta
1901-1903
Listed: 4 December 1997

By building this house for his friend, the sculptor Pierre Braecke (1858–1938), Victor Horta demonstrated his talent for adapting his designs to more modest budgets. Braecke worked with Horta on several occasions, on his own house and Hôtel Solvay.
Braecke had already established his studio in the courtyard of the building block (which has since undergone a transformation) in 1898. After acquiring the land on the street side, he decided to build a house there for himself.
For budgetary reasons, Horta chose not to build a stone façade, but instead clad it with mortar, adding blue stone elements to accentuate its lines, especially around the doors. The entrance door and carriage gate are joined in a stone frame with a very organic design. The façade is arranged around the chimney, which serves as a central axis. It also reveals the interior's simple and functional organisation. The left part of the house is where the actual house is located, with the kitchen in the cellar, and the dining and sitting room on the upper floor. The narrower section, to the right, is where the entrance and stairwell are located. A covered passageway in the wider section leads to the studio. A small design studio is illuminated by the skylight on the second floor.

Horta succeeds in creating a very elegant, albeit pared down façade here, by making good use of the volumes and the contrasting materials. Just take a look at the handle of the carriage gate, which Braecke made, and which also serves as a letterbox. The inscription in Dutch, 'brieven' (letters) is a reminder that Braecke was Flemish, having grown up in Nieuwpoort, a small seaside resort. Horta was also in charge of the interior finish and furniture, which are also simple yet refined.

At no. 4 in Rue de l'Abdication, you can find another one of Gustave Strauven's projects (1902). It is all there: the joyous polychromy of the bricks, the bay window, with a balcony above it, a few stained glass windows and the typical dormer flanked by decorative buttresses, that form an arch that is slightly horseshoe-shaped, which reminds us of the top of the Saint Cyr house (listed on 30 April 2006).

House of the sculptor Pierre Braecke ▶

8/ HOUSE OF THE ARCHITECT GUSTAVE STRAUVEN

RUE LUTHER 28 / RUE CALVIN 5, 1000 BRUSSELS

Architect: Gustave Strauven
1902
Classement: 6 mai 2004

In 1902, Gustave Strauven bought a corner lot, immediately selling the extremity of it, choosing to keep the narrow curved part, that was only 3.75 metres wide, for himself, to build his house on it. Its narrowness is offset by the sheer brilliance of Strauven's architectural design, both on the inside and outside. In many ways, it is similar to the Saint Cyr house, which was nearing completion at the time.

The façade features a series of large windows, that are flanked by two yellow and blue brick pilasters, accentuated with carved white stone elements. The entrance, which closes with a cast iron gate, with an arabesque motif surmounted by wrought iron scrolls, is most original and reminds us of the town houses at the seaside. A staircase in a large loggia leads to the upper floor, with another leading to the kitchen in the cellar. This loggia is accentuated in the façade by a masonry arch that was built on a curved steel profile. The upper part of the arch has been left open, so the light can fall in on the upper floor. On the first floor, the protruding bay window offsets the fact that the ground-floor is set back. A few years ago, there was no bay window but as the owner had the original plans, in which it was included, he was able to add it in place of a balcony. On the uppermost floor, the dormer has been incorporated in the roof with its attic rooms. The

28

roof is surmounted by two pinnacles, to which the cast iron railings of the roof terrace are affixed.
The façade at the rear, in Rue Calvin, is set back, above a garage that was built in place of the small yard that used to be here in the Twenties. The three floors, of decreasing height, have large windows, with terraces or balconies.
The interior is organised around the central, pentagonal stairwell, with a small skylight, which gives access, on each floor, to a room at the front and the rear of the house.
The house's owner, Olivier Berckmans, was in charge of the long restoration process.

PORTRAIT: OLIVIER BERCKMANS

Olivier Berckmans lives in the house that Gustave Strauven built for himself in 1902. The art historian, who studied restoration and conservation of architectural and urban heritage, previously worked for the Heritage Department of the Regional Public Service of Wallonia. He is currently employed with the Association pour l'Étude du Bâti (APEB)[3], which is tasked with establishing an inventory of Brussels' architectural heritage, which carries out historical research about buildings and raises the public's awareness about heritage through exhibitions, publications, and guided visits.

Cécile Dubois: How did you become the owner of this house?
Olivier Berckmans: I had been familiar with Strauven's work since the Seventies, when I was in charge of establishing an inventory of the heritage in Tournai, where he built several houses around 1904–1905. At the end of the Nineties, when I was interested in buying a house, somebody mentioned this one to me. While I was looking for a more classical style, I thought the house looked so beautiful despite its rundown condition that I considered it a unique opportunity to reconnect with Strauven. I lived there from the outset, which was far from easy as it urgently needed restoring. I had the original plans at my disposal although I also knew that Strauven tended to take a lot of liberties and stray from his original design. I started by renovating the interior, which had been completely partitioned. I then undertook the restoration of the façade in two phases. I started with the façade itself and then added the bay window, which had never been built. We don't know for sure whether there ever was a bay window. Some neighbours told there used to be one. In my opinion, it was never built, for budgetary reasons, even though Strauven had drawn one. Now it feels as if it has always been there, as the protruding bay window offsets the ground floor, which is slightly set back. We re-established an equilibrium in Strauven's design.

CD: What do you think are the main characteristics of Gustave Strauven's architecture?
OB: Strauven used the contrast between the protruding volumes (bow windows, bay windows, balconies, etc.) and the set back volumes (loggia) in the most amazing way in the façades of his best designs. He used multiple reliefs for the surfaces, working with lesenes (low-relief vertical pilaster strips), which are joined by arcatures. He combined bricks in different colours, which added vibrancy to his designs. The ironwork also enhances this visually stunning spectacle. His façades are like large altarpieces, culminating in a crowning flourish.
At first glance, it may look a little over the top, but look closer and you will discover that there is a real logic to his design.

CD: What makes living in this house so charming?
OB: As you find yourself in between two façades that are made up of a succession of window frames, the interior is very light. You can be outside on the terrace of the loggia on the upper floor,

while still feeling as though you are inside. Strauven liked to play with this ambiguity. What's more, there is a decorative moulding on the outside wall, which continues inside. The roof is conceived like a terrace and Strauven had reason to do so as the façade is surmounted by a cast iron railing. There is no heavy cornice that impedes the façade's elevation. On the contrary, the façade seems to extend forever, blending in with the sky. The bricks also enhance this effect. In the base of the façade, yellow bricks are the dominant material, while the blue bricks seem to be added as an afterthought. As you move up the façade, the colour scheme is inverted.

CD: What do we know about Gustave Strauven's personality?

OB: Not much really. Strauven continues to be a mystery. He did not marry, had no children, and died young. Until recently, we had no idea what he looked like even. We now know thanks to the photo in his military passbook[4]. We also know that he never actually lived in the house, as he immediately rented it out. We had his handwriting analysed by a graphologist, who concluded that he was very self-assured.

He often was in hot water with the authorities because of his projects because they did not comply with the urban planning rules. Strauven never really understood why he was subjected to such proceedings as he considered himself a talented architect. He was an excellent designer, especially of ironwork. The APEB has created an entire site that is dedicated to his work, which lists over eighty projects and achievements, including plans, photos, and analyses.

The online platform **Bruxelles, Ville d'Architectes** (www.villedarchitectes.brussels) will at some point become the portal for all sites about Brussels' architects. The first one is dedicated to Gustave Strauven: **www.gustavestrauven.brussels.**

At 85, Boulevard Clovis, the Van Dyck house (Gustave Strauven, 1900) stands out because of its two very different spans. The right span is set back, while the left span, of which the orientation changes slightly on the upper floor, is designed in relief. Each floor is extended with a balcony. The two upper balconies are connected by an inclined metal flagpole, that resembles the mast of a boat. The gable is surmounted by a small loggia, which originally should have had a dome on top of it, with ironwork as a finishing touch (listed on 8 August 1988).

9/ QUAKER HOUSE

SQUARE AMBIORIX 50, 1000 BRUSSELS

Architect: Georges Hobé
1899
Listed: 9 February 2006

Georges Hobé (1854–1936) originally worked as a carpenter and came to architecture relatively late in life, teaching himself everything. A staunch defender of the English cottage, designed as a model of constructive logic and domestic comfort, which also blended in with its surroundings, Hobé built several villas at the seaside and in Namur. Horta writes that he unintentionally influenced Hobé's career as an architect.[5] Hobé, who worked exclusively as a carpenter at the time, recommended Horta as an architect to one of his clients, Georges Deprez. Horta was not aware of this, however, and failed to contact him for the woodwork in the house. Hobé was incensed, and therefore decided to offer his own services as an architect to his clients. This house, which is much simpler in style than anything we have seen so far, is inspired by the English cottage style for the exterior (with bow windows, a monumental chimney, and a slate roof) and by Art Nouveau for the interior.

The façade contrasts red brick with white stone and has a monumental bow-window on the corner, which significantly expands the interior space, offering nice views of the outside.

The house, which was originally built for a currency exchange broker, the house is now home to the offices of the Quaker Council for European affairs.

10/ HÔTEL VAN EETVELDE AND APARTMENT BUILDING

AVENUE PALMERSTON 2-4, 1000 BRUSSELS

Architect: Victor Horta
1895-1901
Listed: 21 June 1971 and 10 April 2008 (no. 2): 18 November 1976 and 10 April 2008 (no. 4)
Listed as UNESCO World Heritage since 2000

▲ Hôtel van Eetvelde, avenue Palmerston 4

Edmond van Eetvelde (1852–1925) was an atypical client for Horta. He was not an industrialist. In 1886, he returned to Belgium after a long career in China and India, where he served as consul. King Leopold II appointed him as administrator general of foreign affairs of the Congo Free State and in 1894, he became the Secretary of state of the independent state of Congo. He was tasked with implementing the King's Congo policy and with organising the harvest of rubber and the collection of ivory. As a prominent civil servant, he turned to Horta for the construction of his mansion. In his *Mémoires*, Horta discusses their initial meetings and describes van Eetvelde as a man 'who had the nervousness, which the king required from anyone who chose to serve him'.[6] His request was as follows: 'I want a house for my family. I have the same needs as everyone else. I need to receive people so I need at least a large salon and a dining room that is just as large as you can make it[7]...'. The two men got on well, which is why Horta decided to 'propose the boldest possible design'[8] he ever made. Mrs van Eetvelde was more difficult to convince however. She felt that 'modernism [means] people',[9] perhaps confusing Art Nouveau with the Maison du Peuple, which was being built at the time. The Hôtel van Eetvelde and its extensions is a unique ensemble as it shows how much and how rapidly the architect's style evolved by the end of the nineteenth century. Initially, Horta was asked to build the mansion at no. 4, which he designed in 1895. By 1899, van Eetvelde had bought the land to the left at no. 2, and asked Horta to extend his mansion and build a house so that he could rent out on the land. In 1901, Horta added another span to the mansion, to the right, which extended across half of the land (the other half had been sold to the neighbour).

The façade at no. 4, which was built during the first phase (1895), is very innovative. The only skeleton-façade in Horta's career projects outwards on the two first floors. Even though it is painted orange, the metal structure is clearly visible, and the rivets even become a decorative feature. Under the windows, the sills have been decorated with mosaics, in the whiplash style. The garden gate is probably one of the architect's most exuberant designs.

Horta's Art Nouveau style was considerably toned down in the extension of 1899 and the rental house. The steel structure is no longer visible on the façade. The first span, to the left of the mansion, is similar to the extension, and has a study on the upper floor. The rental house which extends towards square Marie-Louise has a monumental porch. From 1920 onwards, the extension and the rental house were combined. The interior was redone in 1958. The annex of 1901, to the right of the hotel, was designed in a more classical style, almost without any Art Nouveau references.

Inside, the decorative scheme blends in with the structure in the most exceptional way. The 32-metre long building has a front volume, a central volume, a light shaft that illuminates the winter garden, and another volume at the rear. The reception rooms are on the first floor and the owner's private apartments on the second and third floors. The servants' quarters are on the ground floor and in the attic (bedrooms).

On the ground floor, which is not very high, the walls of the entrance hall are clad with bands of pink and white marble. The hall leads to the servants' quarters. Behind the bevelled glass door, the mosaic floor staircase on the diagonal, in shades of green and orange, spirals around the octagonal winter garden. The architect has succeeded in creating an architectural promenade in the centre of the house. By creating detours, he gives the impression that the house is much larger than it is in reality.

On the upper floor, an open gallery winds it way around the winter garden, which is covered with a monumental stained glass window, supported by eight metal pillars. From there you can walk into the sitting room, at the front of the house or the dining room at the back of the house. The decoration of the dining room refers to Africa. Some of the doors are decorated with American glass windows.

Opposite Hôtel van Eetvelde, at no. 3 in Avenue Palmerston, Victor Horta built Hôtel Deprez-Van de Velde for the director of the Crystal Val-Saint-Lambert factory. He wanted to have a place to stay in Brussels (1896). Unfortunately, the building was stripped of most of its Art Nouveau elements during subsequent renovations (listed on 21 June 1971).

At no. 46 in Rue du Cardinal, you can see an eclectic house, which was clearly influenced by Art Nouveau. The house was the result of a brief collaboration between the architects Josse Van Kriekinge and Benjamin De Lestré (1900). A bas-relief on the first floor features an allegory of architecture. It is quite rare to find figurative sculptures on an Art Nouveau façade. Generally, sculptural elements were used for architectural motifs, such as the consoles, keystones, and windowsills. The ironwork of the entrance door and the cellar door evoke a peacock's tail (listed on 28 February 1991).

11/ HOUSES

SQUARE GUTENBERG 5 AND RUE PHILIPPE LE BON 55, 1000 BRUSSELS

Architect: Armand Van Waesberghe
1898
Listed: 22 April 1999 (square Gutenberg); 2 July 1998 (Rue Philippe le Bon)

These two houses are an excellent opportunity to discuss the work of Armand Van Waesberghe (1879–1949), an architect who was a unique individual, a real shooting star! He spent one year at Saint-Luc, but already attracted attention as of 1898, at the age of nineteen, when he built a set of town houses. After 1900, he did not build very much and by 1908 he was no longer working as an architect.

The houses were built for Caroline Schröders, who lived at no. 5 Square Gutenberg on an L-shaped piece of land. They are typical examples of the architect's own personal Art Nouveau style, which was influenced by Paul Hankar. The façades, which are very similar in terms of their composition, are very colourful. Van Waesberge used bricks in various colours, blue stone, stained glass windows, and sgraffiti. The blue stone bases extend upwards, creating a unique frame, with sculpted lines, which are sometimes interrupted by red bricks, for the front doors and their transom window and for the cellar windows and the large horseshoe-shaped windows on the upper floor. There is bay window on the first floor of each house, while the second floor has been divided into three narrow windows, which recalls the three dormers at the top of the façade, which look like decorative turrets. The sgraffiti and ironwork, which alternate between sinuous lines and a more geometric design, add a finishing touch.

The references to Gothic architecture, which are so frequent in the architect's work, are evident in the verticality of the houses, and the elongation of the façades. A fun little detail: the scrapers are shaped like lancet arches.

▲ Square Gutenberg 5

Van Waesberge built nine houses in just nine months in the Squares neighbourhood. The floor plan is usually traditional, but the architect also designed the interior, the furniture, and the rugs. In square Gutenberg, he built no. 8 and no. 19. No. 8 is a typical example of his style, but the sgraffiti have not been repainted properly. The composition of the façade at no. 19 is very different (listed on 22 April 1999).

12/ HOUSE OF THE ARCHITECT VICTOR TAELEMANS

RUE PHILIPPE LE BON 70, 1000 BRUSSELS

Architect: Victor Taelemans
1901
Listed: 8 August 1988

Victor Taelemans (1864–1920), who studied at the Academy of Fine Arts of Brussels, worked as a designer for Henri Beyaert, where he met Paul Hankar. From the 1890s onwards, he started to work for himself, initially building eclectic houses. Over time, he moved to the Art Nouveau style, and was clearly influenced by Paul Hankar, Victor Horta, and Octave Van Rysselberghe.
This house is similar to the Hôtel Otlet, which Van Rysselberghe built in 1896 (see p. 21). You can feel that Taelemans's design, in an upper middle class neighbourhood, on a corner parcel moreover, was intentional. The architect wanted his work to be seen.
The house is very simple and its geometric style striking.
A round window is subdivided into rectangles, while the entrance door is incorporated in a circle. The bay windows on the first floor are trapezoidal, rectangular, and triangular.
The façade's composition is indicative of its interior. The architect's large office is situated to the right of the entrance door. It is illuminated by four windows and a small waiting room to the left. The dining room is situated at the rear, with a round window in the façade. The central part of the ground-floor is occupied by a vast staircase. On the first floor, the bay windows extend the living areas, the large sitting room, and the smoking room. The largest of the bedrooms on the second floor, on the corner, has a small balcony.
The façade in white Euville and Savonniàres stone, originally featured sgraffiti, under the cornice.
The entrance door was incorporated into a stone arch, with two small whiplash elements, which recalled Horta's style.
Many of the original elements of the interior, which was restored in 2011–2013, were retained.
In 1907, Victor Taelemans built a new house and studio for himself, in Rue Ernest Solvay in Ixelles (see p. 98).

ZONE
30

FIFTH WALK

IXELLES
FROM SAINT-BONIFACE TO THE IXELLES PONDS AND AVENUE LOUISE

During this rather long walk you will discover the neighbourhoods of Ixelles to the east of Avenue Louise—the more commercial Saint-Boniface district—and the area around the ponds of Ixelles, which is more residential. Groups of buildings by Delune, Blerot, and Jacobs are included, as are 'portrait houses', built for famous clients by Victor Horta or Octave van Rysselberghe and Henry van de Velde.

◂ Detail of the façade, rue Ernest Solvay 20, Ernest Blerot, 1900-1901

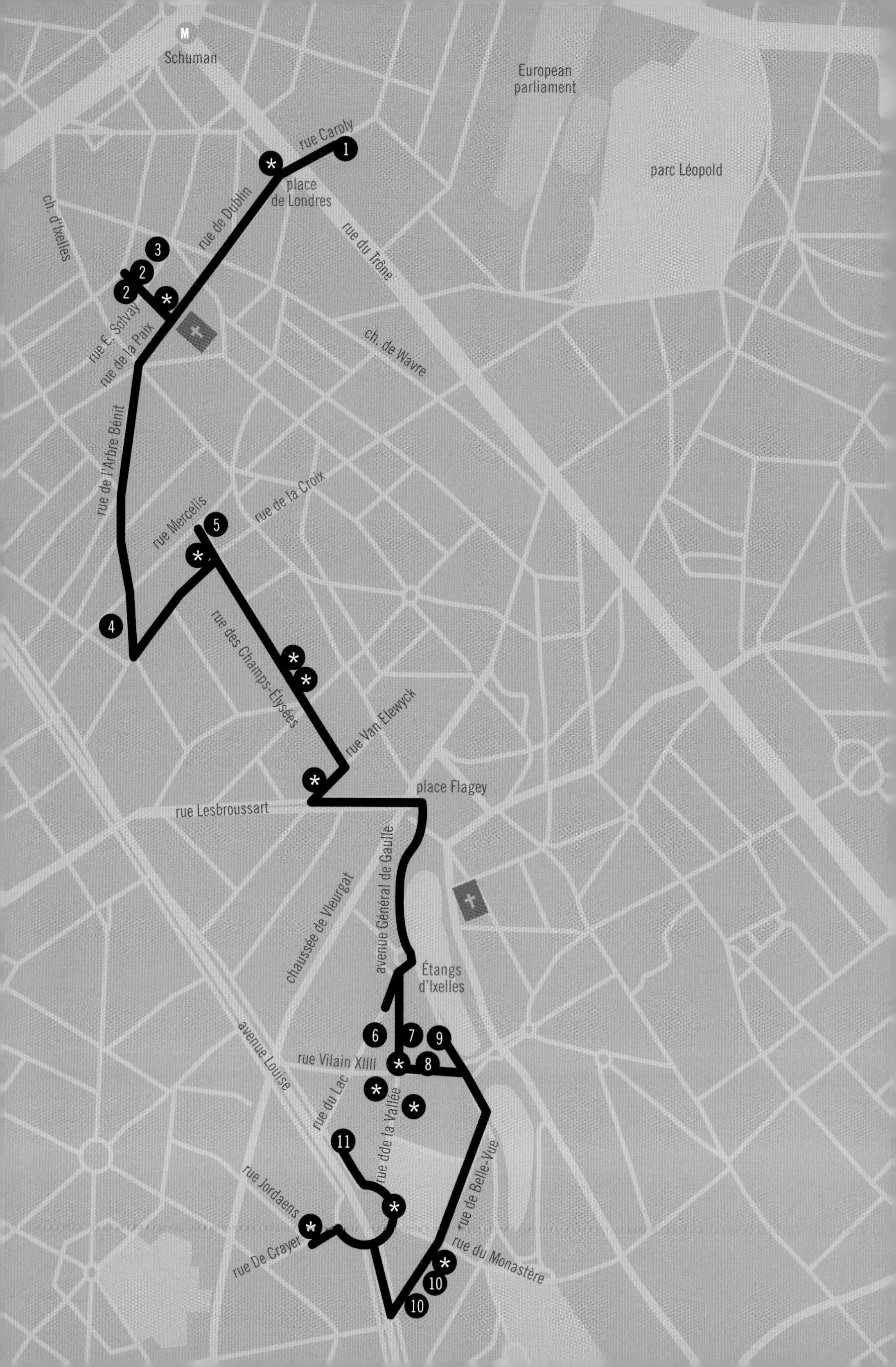
Schuman
European parliament
parc Léopold
rue Caroly
place de Londres
rue de Dublin
rue du Trône
ch. d'Ixelles
rue E. Solvay
rue de la Paix
ch. de Wavre
rue de l'Arbre Bénit
rue de la Croix
rue Mercelis
rue des Champs-Élysées
rue Van Elewyck
place Flagey
rue Lesbroussart
avenue Général de Gaulle
chaussée de Vleurgat
Étangs d'Ixelles
avenue Louise
rue Vilain XIIII
rue du Lac
rue dde la Vallée
rue de Belle-Vue
rue Jordaens
rue De Crayer
rue du Monastère

01 **SIMOENS HOUSE**
RUE CAROLY 19, 1050 IXELLES

02 **GROUP OF ELEVEN HOUSES**
RUE SAINT-BONIFACE 15-19 AND 20-22 AND
RUE ERNEST SOLVAY 12-22 AND 19, 1050 IXELLES

03 **HOUSE OF THE ARCHITECT VICTOR TAELEMANS**
RUE ERNEST SOLVAY 32, 1050 IXELLES

04 **HOUSE OF THE ARCHITECT PAUL SAINTENOY**
RUE DE L'ARBRE BÉNIT 123, 1050 IXELLES

05 **HOUSE OF ÉDOUARD TAYMANS**
RUE DES CHAMPS-ÉLYSÉES 6, 1050 IXELLES

06 **HOUSE**
RUE DU LAC 6, 1050 IXELLES

07 **HOUSES**
RUE DE LA VALLÉE 2 TO 28, 32 AND 36, 1050 IXELLES

08 **GROUP OF TWO HOUSES**
RUE VILAIN XIIII 9 AND 11, 1050 IXELLES

09 **GROUP OF TWO HOUSES**
AVENUE GÉNÉRAL DE GAULLE 38 AND 39,
1050 IXELLES

10 **HOUSES**
RUE DE BELLE-VUE 30, 32 AND 42 TO 46, 1050 IXELLES

11 **HÔTEL MAX HALLET**
AVENUE LOUISE 346, 1050 BRUSSELS

1/ SIMOENS HOUSE
RUE CAROLY 19, 1050 IXELLES
Architect: Henri Jacobs
1904
Listed: 15 June 2006

Rue Caroly is located in the neo-classical Leopold district, which was developed from 1837 onwards. This Art Nouveau house is an exception, but it was also built much later, in 1904. Often mistakenly referred to as Hôtel Baron Buffin (who lived at no. 17 in reality), the house was built by the Schaerbeek architect Henri Jacobs for Marie Simoens, who was also from Schaerbeek. The very specious house was designed for an occupant who practiced a liberal profession, with a cabinet and two waiting rooms on the ground floor. A monumental staircase leads to the adjoining rooms on the first floor.

As is often the case with Henri Jacobs, the composition of the façade is very balanced and the floors are subtly connected by architectural elements. On the ground floor, the two spans are flanked by moulded pilasters, which fan out upwards, extending into the consoles of the first-floor balcony and the cylindrical pillars of the railing. The two large windows on the first floor are framed by slender stone columns that blend into the extremities of the second-floor balcony. The beautiful house features several refined details: the ironwork, the carved white and blue stone with its plant motifs, the decorative panels, and the sgraffiti.

At 65, Rue du Trône, at the corner of Place de Londres, the eclectic apartment building has a remarkable Art Nouveau storefront that was built in 1906 for a bakery, which was subsequently occupied by the fishmonger of the Léopold neighbourhood in 1926. While it is very similar in style to Paul Hankar's work, it cannot be attributed to him. The upper part of the windows and the transom of the entrance are decorated with wood frames with geometric patterns. Inside, the wall behind the counter is covered with a large ceramic panel featuring a fishing scene. The panel, which was produced by Helman, is almost identical to one of the panels of Restaurant Vincent in the city centre (see p. 163à) (storefront listed on 18 March 2004).

At no. 7 to no. 11 in Rue Saint-Boniface, Henri Jacobs built three apartment buildings with storefronts for three sisters, called Marie, Céline, and Martha Simoens. While they are more modest than the house in Rue Caroly, they undeniably have certain architectural qualities. Combining brick with blue stone or brick with white stone, their façades have windows in various shapes. The entresol of nos. 7 and 11 have butterfly-shaped windows, a common feature in Jacobs's work.

2/ GROUP OF ELEVEN HOUSES

RUE SAINT-BONIFACE 15-19 AND 20-22 AND RUE ERNEST SOLVAY 12-22 AND 19, 1050 IXELLES

Architect: Ernest Blerot
1900-1901
Listed: 5 March 1998

Rue Saint-Boniface is the backbone of a neighbourhood that developed in the late nineteenth century, along the axis of the eponymously-named church (Joseph Jonas Dumont, 1846–1849). Upon completion of the roadworks in 1900, commercial buildings were built along the main arteries, including these eleven Art Nouveau buildings by the architect Ernest Blerot at the intersection with Rue Ernest Solvay.

Blerot started building this group of buildings around the same time that he built the first houses on Rue Vanderschrick in Saint-Gilles (see p. 66). Hence, this was a particularly prolific period for the architect. To save time, he used identical façade elements, as you can see if you compare the two groups of buildings.

The buildings, which were built on similar lots of land, have many characteristics in common: they have three floors and two or three spans, a storefront on the ground floor and the home of the trader on the upper floors. The stairwell is on the side of the building, with adjoining rooms on every floor.

The corner buildings are slightly different and have an apartment on each floor. The stairwells are visible in the façade, in a span with staggered windows.

The brick façades look lively because of the bands of stone, and all have their own individual identity because of architectural and decorative details, which are inspired from nature or medieval architecture (pinnacles, gables, broken bows…). The façades of the two corner buildings have superimposed wooden bay windows, that are reminiscent of the watchtowers of medieval castles. Once again Blerot demonstrates the extent of his imagination, in the design of the wrought iron, the window frames, the entrance doors, the sgraffiti, and so on.The overall impression is one of harmony and these façades have generally been well preserved, despite the addition of or the disappearance of some sgraffiti.

Rue Saint-Boniface 19 and 17 ▼

3/ HOUSE OF THE ARCHITECT VICTOR TAELEMANS

RUE ERNEST SOLVAY 32, 1050 IXELLES

Architect: Victor Taelemans
1904
Listed: 19 February 1998

▲ Photo published in *Vers l'Art*, 1909, pl. 27

Around 1907, Victor Taelemans left Rue Philippe le Bon (see page 90) for this neighbourhood, which was then in full expansion, moving into a house with an original façade. Unfortunately, it suffered over time and the Art Nouveau window frames on the ground floor were replaced by storefronts in 1965. Let us hope the house will one day be restored to its former glory.

The house refers to the work of Octave Van Rysselberghe and Victor Horta, using white stone for the façade, which is elegantly carved. The way in which the bay windows are grafted onto the façade, however, recalls Paul Hankar's style. The decorative vocabulary, especially the ironwork of the entrance door or the railing of the second-floor railing and the design of the window frame all refer to the geometric Art Nouveau style. The entrance door has been incorporated in a horseshoe-shaped arch.

The main rooms in this shallow house are all located at the front of the house. Originally, the ground floor was used by an architect's practice, while the dining room was to the left. The sitting rooms were on the upper floor. Many of the original interesting details have been retained.

At 52, Rue Souveraine, you can see a typical façade by Gustave Strauven (1899). The Art Nouveau style is mainly evident in the consoles and the wrought iron railings, in the woodwork of the entrance door and the transom of the window, as well as in the sgraffiti, including the one bearing the name 'Villa Kjobenhavn'. The roof was altered in 1989.

4/ HOUSE OF THE ARCHITECT PAUL SAINTENOY

RUE DE L'ARBRE BÉNIT 123, 1050 IXELLES

Renovated in 1897 by the architect Paul Saintenoy
Listed: 2 July 1992

The façade of this house is not an Art Nouveau façade but has been built in the eclectic style, with references to the Italian Renaissance. Built in 1872, it was bought, renovated and transformed for personal use by the architect Paul Saintenoy in 1897. Nowadays, it belongs to the Hungarian Catholic Mission.

Paul Saintenoy, who designed the Old England department store, an emblematic Art Nouveau building (see page 167), also took a keen interest in restoration, continuing to build in historicist styles. This is obvious in the interior of his own home, in which he combined eclectic elements, some of which have been reclaimed, with Art Nouveau. The most remarkable feature is the stained glass window that adorns the large street-side window of the large sitting room. *La Vague* ('The wave') was produced by Raphaël Evaldre after a cartoon by Privat Livemont, who was inspired by a print by the Japanese master Hokusai (1830 or 1831). The naiad in the centre of the composition, with her clasped hands and closed eyes, and whose undulating locks are punctuated with seaweed and shells, is struggling against the rough waves. The violence of the scene contrasts with the soothing linearity of the clouds in the upper part of the stained glass window.

Raphael Evaldre (1862–1868), who was born in Lille and studied at the Ecole des Beaux-Arts in Paris, established a reputation for himself as a creator of stained glass windows in Brussels in 1892 or 1893, when Art Nouveau was just emerging. His name is associated with some of the most beautiful Art Nouveau buildings in Brussels, including those of Victor Horta (Hôtel van Eetvelde, Hôtel Solvay, etc.). He was one of the first glass artists to work in the American glass that was developed in the 1880s in the United States by Tiffany and Lafarge. This type of glass is used in every one of Victor Horta's buildings. Combining molten glass with metallic oxides, this opalescent glass can be used for optimal effect, both indoors and out, and is pretty to look at from both sides.

At 25, Rue de la Croix, we walk past the former workshop of the painter and decorator Géo Ponchon. This artisan specialised in sgraffiti with bird and foliage motifs, as you can gather from the decorations on the façade.
Monique Cordier restored the sgraffiti in 2010.

▼ House of the architect Paul Saintenoy
▼ Detail of the stained glass window, entitled *La Vague*

5/ HOUSE OF ÉDOUARD TAYMANS
RUE DES CHAMPS-ÉLYSÉES 6, 1050 IXELLES

Architect: Paul Hamesse
1906 and 1912
Listed: 14 March 1996

In 1906 and later in 1912, Édouard Taymans, a coal merchant who made his fortune marketing a burner of his own invention, entrusted Paul Hamesse with the task of transforming his nineteenth-century eclectic-style home into a building with a home, a showroom, warehouses, and offices in a geometric Art Nouveau style that was heavily influenced by the Viennese Secession.

The composition of the house's façade, on the street side, is reminiscent of the older building, but Hamesse added a square corner turret with a loggia. The stone capital of the corner pillar of the turret is carved with geometric patterns. In 1940, the brick cladding of the first two floors replaced the original painted plaster. Between the first and the second floor, a ceramic frieze features alternating motifs of plant wreaths and miner's lamps, referring to the origins of the merchant's fortune. Finally, the upper part of the façade is decorated with enamelled bricks, in green, yellow, and plum.

The handle of the entrance door, in which the letterbox has been incorporated, is similar to that of other projects by the architect.

The offices and warehouses were located in the rear building, at the other end of the courtyard and could be accessed through the large glass showroom where the burners were on display. The gallery has an exposed metallic structure that is grafted onto a carved blue stone base. The entrance is framed by two stone pillars and surmounted by a blue stone bas-relief by the sculptor Victor Rousseau, which represents fire. This bas-relief points to Taymans's interest in the arts. As a patron of the arts, he distributed plaster replicas of works purchased from artists such as Constantin Meunier or Godefroid Devreese to his workers and customers.

At 72, Rue des Champs-Elysées the Ludwig house has been restored to its former glory. It was built by Paul Hamesse in 1908. Two sgraffiti in ochre hues with plant motifs decorate the entrance span.

The architect Léon Delune built the adjoining group of buildings at no. 74 Rue des Champs-Élysées and at nos. 21, 23, and 25 in Rue Hennin, for himself (he lived at no. 21). The houses are characterised by the different shapes of the windows, several of which have a horseshoe-shaped arch and by the sgraffiti that were produced by Paul Cauchie.

The architect Aimable Delune, Léon's brother, lived at no. 41, Rue van Elewyck, in a house that was built in 1903. The sills of the bay window are decorated with sgraffiti, which feature the year in which the house was built and the monograms of the owners: AD and CV, for Aimable Delune and Catherine Varvenne. The tympanum of the large flared stone arch above the metallic lintel of the triple windows, on the second floor, is decorated with a sgraffito representing a vase containing plants. The dominant red of the sgraffiti contrasts with the whiteness of the glazed bricks and the stone (listed on 23 February 2006). The same architect built the two neighbouring houses, at 43 and 45, Rue Van Elewijck in 1902.

6/ HOUSE

RUE DU LAC 6, 1050 IXELLES

Architect: Ernest Delune
1902
Listed: 23 October 2003

This small façade, one of the most characteristic façades of the Brussels Art Nouveau style, is currently being restored.

Behind it we can make out a stairwell, which is illuminated by a large skylight with a stained glass window, which leads to the artist's studio on the top floor. The whole façade has literally been grafted onto an older, eclectic building, whose entrance was originally located at 5, Rue de la Vallée. The owner wished to enlarge and modernise the building, which is why he called on Ernest Delune, in 1902, who designed a new façade in place of the small triangular courtyard.

The entrance door and its small side window, which are separated by a small stone column, are joined by an elegant circle of stone and decorated with stained glass windows whose patterns blend in harmoniously with the circle around them.

The architectural circle pattern is repeated in the upper part of the main window. The stained glass windows are most likely the work of Clas Grüner Sterner, a master glassworker of Austrian origin, who lived in the house and who collaborated on several occasions with Ernest Delune. They are executed in American glass.

The Delune brothers (Ernest, Léon, Aimable, Edmond, Firmin, and Henri, who were the sons of an entrepreneur from Marbais) and their brother-in-law and cousin (Émile) all were architects or entrepreneurs. Their careers took off just at the time that new neighbourhoods were developed to the south of Brussels. Together they built about one hundred buildings, houses, villas, and apartment buildings, in the eclectic or Art Nouveau style, often designing groups of buildings. The elder brothers—Ernest (1859–1947), Leon (1862–1947), and Aimable (1866–1923)—studied architecture at the Academy of Fine Arts in Brussels before starting to build houses in the eclectic style in the 1890s. From 1900, they turned to Art Nouveau, each succeeding in developing their own take on the style, despite several shared characteristics. As they often built houses in the same neighbourhoods, and even on the same streets buildings are often attributed erroneously. Leon is credited with the extraordinary villa, often called Delune Castle, built from 1904 onwards at 86, Avenue Franklin Roosevelt, on the corner of Avenue des Phalènes (1000 Brussels).

7/ HOUSES

RUE DE LA VALLÉE 2 TO 28, 32 AND 36, 1050 IXELLES

Architect: Ernest Delune

1901-1907

The whole of Rue de la Vallée is exceptional as it comprises fifteen houses with different façades. Some were built in the eclectic style with Art Nouveau characteristics while others are firmly Art Nouveau in appearance. The stone façades, or combined brick and stone façades, which are rarer, often have a small front garden. The façades feature bow windows and small balconies, windows in various shapes, stained glass windows, and so on.

The architect usually signed the edifice with his name. At no. 2, at the corner of Avenue Général de Gaulle, the mansion that was built in 1907 stands out because of its remarkable entrance door, with a stoop, which is surmounted by a colourful stained glass transom with a floral motif. On the side of Avenue Général de Gaulle, the east façade has a monumental window that illuminates the main stairwell. The windows, whose shape is reminiscent of that of Rue du Lac, has been decorated with a stained glass window with floral motifs.

No. 18 (1906) has some original ironwork, in the geometric Art Nouveau style. The entrance is surmounted by a transom window with coloured stained glass, under a stone arch with whiplash motif.

No. 32 (1904) stands out because of its striking wrought iron railing that recalls the ironwork of Ernest Blerot's designs. Here the plant motifs are no longer stylised, but more realistic and three-dimensional. The entrance, which is flanked by two pilasters that taper upwards, supporting a small triangular pediment, resembles the door of a temple. It is surmounted by a particular large window with an upper light, set in a horseshoe-shaped arch, which has been decorated with a colourful stained glass window with floral motifs.

Two Art Nouveau apartment buildings stand at the junction of Rue de la Vallée with Rue Vilain XIIII. On the one side, the building with entrance at 17, Rue Vilain XIIII, was the result of the expansion, in 1932, of a mansion and its outbuildings, which were built in 1903 by Ernest Delune. The two buildings on the opposite side of the street, at 31, Rue de la Vallée and 22, Rue Vilain XIIII, are the outcome of the renovation, in 1934, of two town houses that were built in the early 1900s by Ernest Blerot.

At no. 40 Rue de la Vallée, a large façade in enamelled white brick, punctuated with bonds of white and blue stone and decorated with sgraffiti (Ernest Blerot, 1902) turns out to be a quite complex arrangement of very plastic volumes.

The upper left part is capped with an angled gabled roof that accentuated the building's verticality (listed on 10 October 2002).

◄ 32, Rue de la Vallée

8/ GROUP OF TWO HOUSES

RUE VILAIN XIIII 9 AND 11, 1050 IXELLES

Architect: Ernest Blerot

1902

Listed: 15 March 1983 (no. 9) and 10 June 1993 (no. 11)

Built for the architect himself and probably intended for sale or rental, these two houses, one in brick, the other in stone, are typical of Ernest Blerot's style. The façades feature blue stone bonds and a protruding oriel (no. 9) and bay window (no. 11), with a small overhanging terrace.

The richness of their decoration, however, makes them even more exceptional: the line of the wrought iron grilles which have been designed in a naturalistic way, the joinery of the doors and windows, the finesse of such carved details as the console of the bay window at no. 11 cubicle, the sgraffiti, and the stained glass.

Further down the street, at the corner of the present-day Avenue Général de Gaulle, Ernest Blerot built his own mansion, from 1901 to 1908, also incorporating the offices of his firm in the building. Unfortunately, the building was demolished in 1962 and replaced by a small apartment building.

9/ GROUP OF TWO HOUSES

AVENUE GÉNÉRAL DE GAULLE 38 AND 39, 1050 IXELLES

Architect: Ernest Blerot
1904
Listed: 30 March 1989

While these houses look more austere than the architect's other projects which we have seen so far, they are not any less monumental. In fact, quite the opposite. Originally, they were part of a group of four houses, two of which were demolished in 1939 to make way for La Cascade, the large neighbouring apartment building (René Ajoux).

The patterns on the gates were inspired by nature. Each house has a small front garden, that gives access to a curved staircase, with a wrought iron banister with a sinuous shape, leading to an integrated porch. The cellar has a stone projection, with a garage door, flanked on the left by a narrow servant's entrance. Adding a garage to a house as early as 1904 was quite unusual! At the time, cars were still very rare, but the architect, who was also a passionate mechanic, already foresaw that they would become very popular. These garages are too narrow for today's cars however. The wrought iron railings of the terraces are among the architect's most accomplished and feature clematis leaves, represented in three dimensions in such a detailed manner that they give the illusion of reality. The narrow, low-arched windows (the arch is lower than a semicircle), lends a certain sense of verticality to the façade, just like the gabled dormer at no. 38. This verticality evokes the neo-Gothic, which this Art Nouveau architect, who studied at Saint-Luc, liked a lot.

He has used neither stained glass, nor sgraffiti. The building is all about the austerity and plasticity of the white stone. The floors of the entrance porches and reception areas, on the upper floor, have been decorated with the flowering creepers of clematis. Currently no. 39 is a Bed & Breakfast, called Maison Flagey (www.maisonflagey.com).

At 30, Rue du Monastère, Ernest Blerot built a house in 1900, which was renovated in 1947. The awning at the entrance has been retained. Its wrought iron consoles blend in beautifully with the ramp of the small staircase that leads to the front door, like a metaphor for a vine.

10/ HOUSES
RUE DE BELLE-VUE 30, 32 AND 42 TO 46, 1050 IXELLES
Architect: Ernest Blerot
1897-1900

Ernest Blerot built these houses for various clients. The façades at nos. 30 and 32 (1900) have been skilfully designed to look different, using bricks in different colours. The woodwork, which is very professional, has been retained for the most part or redone, to look identical to the original. The woodwork at no. 30 is more fluid with its stylised plant motifs while the woodwork at no. 32 is more geometric and influenced by Japonism.

Although the façades of no. 42 and no. 44 (1899) are very similar, there are slight differences. The joinery has been altered and repainted. Many of the stained glass windows no longer exist. The windows on the upper floors are gathered in horseshoe-shaped arches. The tympanum of these arches, at no. 42, is decorated with sgraffiti.

The entrance door and the window frames of no. 42 have been replaced.

The transoms on the upper floor of no. 44 is no longer there, but the geometric window frames on the upper floor, which were inspired by Japonism, are still in place.

The bay window at no. 44 was added in 1905, replacing the original balcony.

No. 46 (1898) is slightly older than the other houses and is one of the architect's oldest designs. Blerot built this house under his own name, establishing a reputation for himself as an architect-builder and withholding some of his designs for his own use, to rent or resell them. This façade is also the best-preserved façade of all the buildings. It has a wood and metal bay window and a long vertical window, which is quite unique. It is decorated with a stained glass window with floral motifs, that lets light into the stairwell. The ironwork is particularly expressive: the consoles of the bay window, and the railing on the uppermost floor and the gate that protects the front door stand out in particular.

The sgraffiti have been duly restored. The frame of the large window on the upper floor, with its small wood divisions, with stained glass, has been replaced with a replica of the original.

▲ Rue de Belle-Vue, nos. 42 to 46

On the other side of Avenue Louise, at 34, Rue Jordaens, the De Brouckère hotel, which was designed in 1898 by Octave Van Rysselberghe and Henry van de Velde, has white stone façades on the street side, which rest on a blue stone rubble base. Their regularity and horizontality are remarkable. It is impossible to establish what each architect contributed to the design. In Rue de Crayer, the façade features a balcony with a stone openwork railing, with Japanese motifs, resting on three stone consoles. In Rue Jordaens, the house is extended with a courtyard, surrounded by a wall with gates with a branch motif. The interior is organised around a central hall, with a large open stairwell. Light flows in through a large rectangular skylight with stained glass windows with geometric and floral patterns. The original furniture, which was designed by van de Velde, is no longer in place. It is currently occupied by the offices of the Representation of the German-speaking Community of Belgium to Brussels (listed on 4 December 1997).

Near the roundabout in Avenue Louise, overlooking the King's Gardens (Jardins du Roi) a bronze on a granite pedestal represents the Death of Ompdrailles. The tomb of the wrestlers is a homage to the naturalist writer Léon Cladel and was created by the sculptor Charles Van der Stappen, who worked with the young Victor Horta, who designed the pedestal (1892).

11/ HÔTEL MAX HALLET

AVENUE LOUISE 346, 1050 BRUSSELS

Architect: Victor Horta
1903
Listed: 16 October 1975

This mansion marked a turning point in Horta's career. The façade is elegant and simple. The metal structure is no longer visible and the architect finally abandoned the exuberance of the early Art Nouveau for a more relaxed style. The façade is built entirely in Euville stone and has a certain horizontality to it, which is accentuated by the balcony that extends across the building and the white stone cornice. The details are still very refined, including the way in which Horta used stone: the fluid lines of the ground floor windowsills, the consoles of the balcony, and the modillions of the cornice. The clients were the lawyer and socialist politician Max Hallet (1894–1941), who was a friend of Horta's, and his wife. The mansion was built on land that belonged to Max Hallet's father-in-law.

Inside, the magic takes over, as is always the case in Horta's designs. The layout perfectly fulfilled the clients' requirements. From the carriage way, a few steps lead up to the large hall, the floor of which is decorated with marble mosaics. The main staircase, and the pièce de résistance of the house, is located in this hall. The rooms for the couple's professional and social life are all located on the ground floor: an ante-chamber, an office, a sitting room, and a dining room.

The veined white marble staircase leads to a first landing, which has been transformed into a veranda. Its metal structure contains three arched skylights that let in plenty of light. This space was specifically created for Mrs Hallet, who loved gardening, as you can see from the mural in the stairwell, which was created by a painter-decorator and which depicts climbing roses with plenty of blooms. The stairwell is also lit from above, through a large semi-circular skylight with coloured glass. The first floor is reserved for family life and has a large sitting room, a study, and the master bedroom that overlooks the garden. After World War I, as their conditions changed, the family moved into a new home. 'While my star may have been tarnished, my architecture still shone as brilliantly as before, I think', Horta wrote in his *Memoirs*.[1] The restored house is still inhabited by Mr and Mrs Gilbert, who are great Art Nouveau fans, and their young children.

▾ First landing in the Hôtel Max Hallet

16

SIXTH WALK

A FEW UNKNOWN GEMS IN SAINT-JOSSE-TEN-NOODE AND SCHAERBEEK

FROM THE MUSÉE CHARLIER
TO HÔTEL COHN-DONNAY

This consists of a short walk through the streets of Saint-Josse-ten-Noode and Schaerbeek, where you can discover some rare gems that are almost never included in the major Art Nouveau trails. Some have undergone recent restorations while others are still waiting for an upgrade, which will also allow us to discuss the principles of Heritage protection and grading in the Brussels-Capital Region.

◂ House of the architect Gaston Hayois, avenue Georges Petre 16, 1912

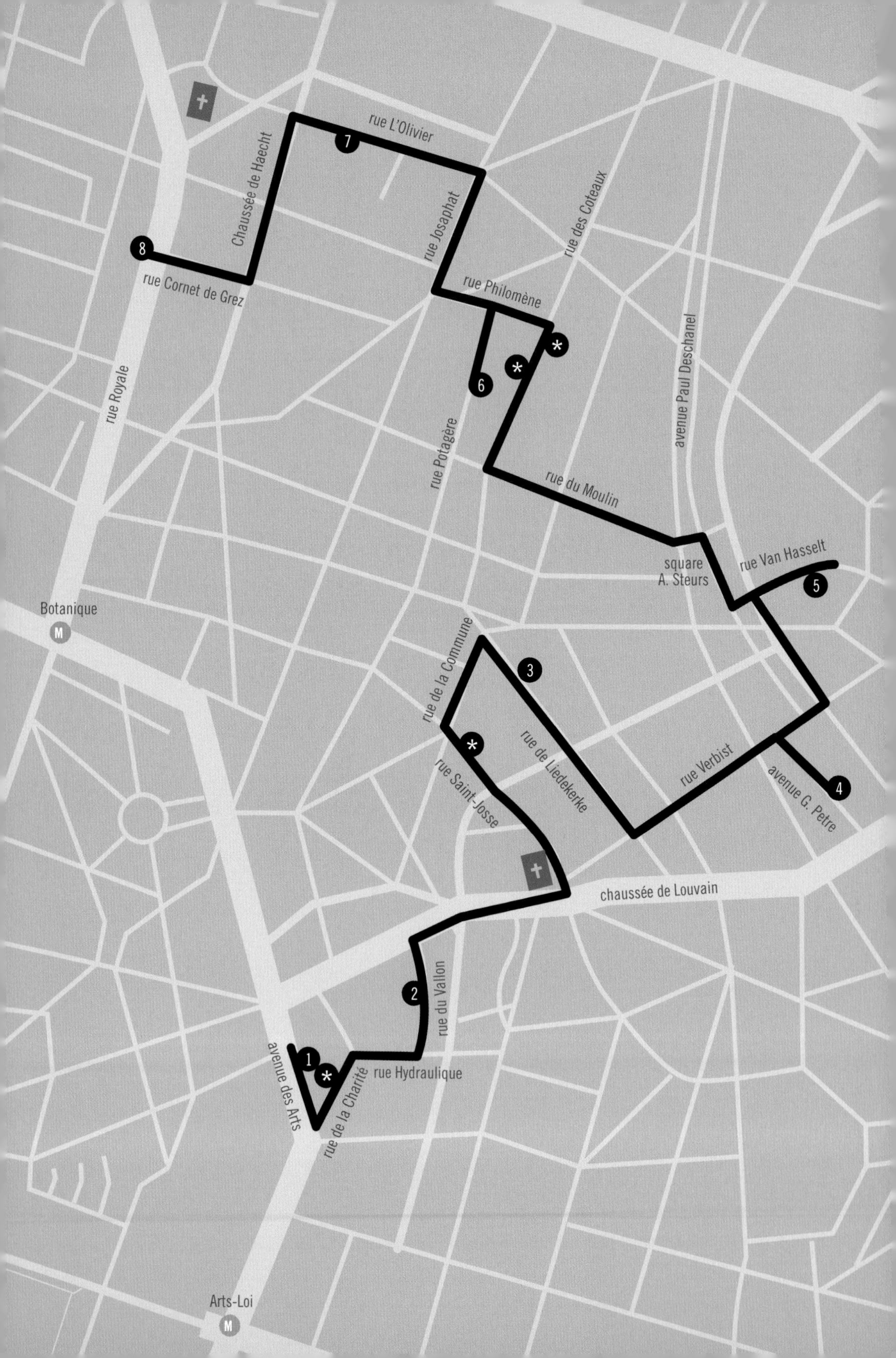

rue L'Olivier
Chaussée de Haecht
rue Josaphat
rue des Coteaux
rue Cornet de Grez
rue Philomène
rue Royale
rue Potagère
avenue Paul Deschanel
rue du Moulin
square
A. Steurs
rue Van Hasselt
Botanique
M
rue de la Commune
rue de Liedekerke
rue Verbist
avenue G. Petre
rue Saint-Josse
chaussée de Louvain
rue du Vallon
avenue des Arts
rue de la Charité
rue Hydraulique
Arts-Loi
M
1
2
3
4
5
6
7
8

01 **CHARLIER MUSEUM**
AVENUE DES ARTS 16, 1210 SAINT-JOSSE-TEN-NOODE

02 **GROUP OF FOUR HOUSES**
RUE DU VALLON 22-28, 1210 SAINT-JOSSE-TEN-NOODE

03 **HOUSE OF THE ARCHITECT LÉON GOVAERTS**
RUE DE LIEDEKERKE 112, 1210 SAINT-JOSSE-TEN-NOODE

04 **GROUP OF HOUSES**
AVENUE GEORGES PETRE 12-16,
1210 SAINT-JOSSE-TEN-NOODE

05 **DEVALCK HOUSE**
RUE ANDRÉ VAN HASSELT 32-34, 1030 SCHAERBEEK

06 **HOUSE AND STUDIO OF THE ARCHITECT MICHEL MAYERES**
RUE POTAGÈRE 150, 1210 SAINT-JOSSE-TEN-NOODE

07 **GROUP OF WORKERS' HOUSES OF FOYER SCHAERBEEKOIS**
RUE L'OLIVIER 16-44, 1030 SCHAERBEEK

08 **HÔTEL COHN-DONNAY**
RUE ROYALE 316, 1210 SAINT-JOSSE-TEN-NOODE

1/ CHARLIER MUSEUM
AVENUE DES ARTS 16, 1210 SAINT-JOSSE-TEN-NOODE
Listed: 15 July 1993

▲ Winter garden at the Charlier Museum

In 1889, Henri Van Cutsem (1839–1904), an art collector and patron of the arts, inherited a neoclassical mansion at 16, Avenue des Arts, tasking Victor Horta, who was still a young architect at the time, with the transformation of the rear of the building into a glazed gallery that could be used as a concert hall or exhibition space. In 1892, Van Cutsem acquired the house next door, which he demolished in order to enlarge his home, a job which he also entrusted to Victor Horta, who combined the new façade with the existing one.

At the rear, Horta built a second glazed gallery or winter garden that connected to the first one. On the ground floor, he created a set of glass shelving units, which created a separation between the smoking room at the front of the house and the sitting room at the back.

While these interventions were not quite Art Nouveau in style, you can already sense that the architect was attempting to create light and transparency. The light from above, which falls in through the skylight, was a harbinger of Horta's future designs. Here he was already using industrial techniques for private homes.

Upon the death of Henri Van Cutsem, his friend, the sculptor Guillaume Charlier (1854–1925) inherited the building, using it as an exhibition space for his own collection. In 1925, Charlier bequeathed the hotel, with its collection, to the Municipality of Saint-Josse-ten-Noode as a public museum. It was inaugurated on 21 October 1928. The collection includes plenty of works from the Belgian school of painting of the late nineteenth century and is definitely worth the detour as part of this Art Nouveau walk. It features portraits, realistic, and Impressionist landscapes, works of a social nature and, finally, works of artists belonging to the innovative movements of the turn of the century, such as James Ensor. The sitting rooms have plenty of Louis XV, Louis XVI, and Empire furniture and decorative art objects as well as tapestries, carpets, porcelain, and silverware.

In all likelihood, Victor Horta became acquainted with Henri Van Cutsem through sculptors, who were his friends and who knew this patron of the arts. They include Guillaume Charlier, Godefroid Devreese, and Charles Van der Stappen. Before he died, Henri Van Cutsem envisaged to bequeath his collection to the City of Tournai which, in exchange, had to commission a museum building from Victor Horta. After the death of his friend, Guillaume Charlier executed this wish and this is how the Museum of Fine Arts of Tournai came about (1903–1928).

At no. 42 Rue de la Charité, you can see the back façade of Hôtel Charlier, which is attributed to Victor Horta. It consists of two distinct parts: on the left, a large façade with a blind elevation in blue stone and Gobertange stone. This is the gallery with its domed glass roof. On the right, you see a section with three floors, in red brick.

2/ GROUP OF FOUR HOUSES

RUE DU VALLON 22-28, 1210 SAINT-JOSSE-TEN-NOODE

Architect: Léon Sneyers
1903
Listed: 14 April 1994

After two decades of poor maintenance and abandonment, despite being listed in 1994, these façades were finally renovated in 2013. They attest to the beginnings of the career of the architect Leon Sneyers, who was influenced by Paul Hankar and the geometric Art Nouveau style. They are different and completely asymmetric, and reflect the architect's concern to create façades with an individual identity, while working on the traditional narrow lots of land in this neighbourhood. The windows are sometimes rounded, sometimes rectangular. The façades have been kept fairly level and simple, with the exception of a bay window and protruding balconies. The ironwork with its geometric motifs, the window frames and joinery, the stained glass, and ceramic tiles with their floral decoration all point to the architect's keen interest in the decorative arts.

At no. 13-15 in Rue Saint-Josse, an Art Nouveau façade from 1902 (Léon Govaerts) features a triangular bow window capped with a balcony with a wrought iron railing. Its form recalls spread wings. Blue stone elements with a plant motif of palmettes and foliage complete the decoration scheme of this original façade.

Rue du Vallon 24-26 ▶

3/ HOUSE OF THE ARCHITECT LÉON GOVAERTS

RUE DE LIEDEKERKE 112, 1210 SAINT-JOSSE-TEN-NOODE

Architect: Léon Govaerts
1899
Listed: 29 June 2000

Léon Jean Joseph Govaerts (1860–1930), was born into a family of decorators, and was himself a talented draughtsman. He left us this beautiful masterpiece, which stands out because of the relaxed style of this ornamental composition, effortlessly switching from Flemish neo-Renaissance to Art Deco and a high quality Art Nouveau.

The façade was the outcome of the transformation, in 1899, of a neo-classical building into the Art Nouveau style that was in vogue at the time. The façade is divided into five fairly narrow spans under a large curved wooden cornice. The central entrance span, which is slightly broader and slightly set back, has a metallic bay window, which rests over the house's entrance.

Sgraffiti with stylised floral motifs, decorative terra cotta ornaments, and the red bricks of the arches around the windows add a dash of colour to the white brick façade. The house, which has been owned by the municipality since 1995, has undergone a radical restoration and is now used by the Maison de la Famille, which offers assistance to the elderly and their families.

The interior is organised around the main vestibule, which is extended by a staircase that is lit by a high window, with a stained glass window representing a vase with flowers. The decoration of the reception rooms on the ground floor is more eclectic in style. The ceiling of the dining room is Art Nouveau in style, while the sitting room tends towards Louis XV.

4/ GROUP OF HOUSES
AVENUE GEORGES PETRE 12-16, 1210 SAINT-JOSSE-TEN-NOODE
Architect: Gaston Hayois
1912

Avenue Georges Petre, with its houses with front gardens and wrought iron gates, looks a little provincial. There are some exceptions but most of the buildings here date from before World War I, and are eclectic in style, with some Art Nouveau elements.

Some buildings that stand out include the buildings of the architect Gaston Hayois:

- Nos. 12 and 14 are symmetrical. Their white façades feature bonds of red brick and blue stone and some unusual mosaic decorations. The overhanging cornices resting on narrow modillions add a picturesque element to their overall appearance;
- No. 16, where the architect lived, is more imposing because of its width, and is divided into three spans. The entrance span is capped with a turret with a balustrade, whose corbelling and consoles evoke the machicolation of a stronghold.

5/ DEVALCK HOUSE
RUE ANDRÉ VAN HASSELT 32-34, 1030 SCHAERBEEK

Architect: Gaspard Devalck
1900
Listed: 4 June 2009

In 1900, Gaspard Devalck succeeded in the endeavour of building a veritable Art Nouveau gem, on a small triangular plot of land. Originally intended for his mother, he decided to establish his practice there instead. It is a typical example of a bourgeois mansion, with an exuberant Art Nouveau decoration, both on the façade and in the interior. The curved façade, with its immaculate design, combines white stone with blue stone bonds and small, narrow red bricks, and has a carved wood cornice. To the right, at no. 32, is the actual house. There is a separate warehouse and dwelling to the left, at no. 34 (in 1902, a tobacco and cigar shop was located here). No. 34 underwent some radical transformations. At No. 32, the window frames are more elaborate and decorated with stained glass, probably manufactured by Raphael Evaldre. These were restored a few years ago and play a major role in the façade's composition, adding a colourful dimension to it. The window of the upper floor represents a heron among reeds while the bay window features a bird and blue irises in pink light, with Japanese-style clouds. The stained glass windows of the other bay window also feature plant motifs.

The upper light of the kitchen in the cellar, with its horseshoe-shaped arch, is protected by a wrought-iron grille with a radiating motif. The front door is surmounted by a sgraffito that is awaiting restoration.

Many of the house's original interior features have been retained, including the stained glass windows which constitute a true hymn to the female body with their sensuous curves.

In 2010, the Municipality of Schaerbeek rewarded the restoration effort with an award.

In 1902, Gaspard Devalck also built the four neighbouring houses, from no. 24 to no. 30, in an eclectic style with Art Nouveau accents.

Gaspard Devalck (1872-1962), who studied at the Brussels Academy, essentially worked in the eclectic style tinged with Art Nouveau elements. Most of his buildings are located in Saint-Josse-ten-Noode, Schaerbeek, and around the neighbourhood of the squares. From 1908, he devoted himself to the construction of the Mosanville estate, near Namur, with villas that combine a picturesque appearance with modern amenities.

In Rue des Coteaux, we find two eclectic groups of houses of Art Nouveau inspiration, which were built by architects who already lived in the neighbourhood. They are almost carbon copies of nearby buildings. It proves that architects did not hesitate to copy their own work or even each other's work, during this intense period of construction!

At nos. 58 and 60, the two houses (Maurice Dechamps, 1900) were built for a contractor.

There was a stable and a large warehouse on the block. The shapes of the stone arches over the windows and doors are original. At no. 60, the arches with archivolt end in a whiplash, while most of the arches at no. 58 are serrated on the outside. On the other side of Rue des Coteaux, at 53–55 and 57–59, two apartment buildings with a storefront on the ground floor, mirror each other (Dominique Fastré, 1907), and are very similar in appearance to two buildings built the previous year by Gustave Strauven at 334–340 Rue Josaphat. The polychromy that is created by using bricks in different colours is also typical of Strauven's style. The sgraffiti on the façades have been preserved and feature floral motifs and women's faces

▼ Stained glass window of the bay window, Devalck house

6/ HOUSE AND STUDIO OF ARCHITECT THE MICHEL MAYERES

RUE POTAGÈRE 150, 1210 SAINT-JOSSE-TEN-NOODE

Architect: Michel Mayeres
1904
Listed: 12 March 1998

The entrepreneur and architect Michel Mayeres, who built several rather eclectic apartment buildings in the neighbourhood, here built a building to satisfy a whim! This was his own home of course. The blue stone base of the façade flares out, and is properly anchored in the soil. The ground floor and first floor are divided vertically into four spans, with windows grouped two by two in the same stone frame, which add a vertical dimension to the edifice.

The slightly broken arches that surround the first floor windows are of Moorish influence, whereas the railings of these windows as well as the balcony above the door are more similar in style to the geometric Art Nouveau.

On the second floor, the two central spans merge to form an impressive bow-window, under the large curved central bay window on the third floor (combining curve and counter-curve) of the architect's studio. This window is surrounded by a radiant transom with wood divisions in a horseshoe arch. The ochre plastering of the upper levels replaced the sgraffito which did not stand the test of time. The composition of the upper part of the façade, with its rounded window and its sgraffiti, is reminiscent of the architecture of Paul Hankar, more specifically of the Hôtel Ciamberlani (see page 18).

7/ GROUP OF WORKERS' HOUSES OF FOYER SCHAERBEEKOIS

RUE L'OLIVIER 16-44, 1030 SCHAERBEEK

Architect: Henri Jacobs

1903

Foyer Schaerbeekois, the first housing authority of its kind in Belgium, was founded on 2 February 1899. Its purpose was to 'build, buy, sell, and rent dwellings for the working classes.'[1] After winning a competition for the construction of workers' houses, the architect Henri Jacobs soon became the go-to architect for the housing authority, attending meetings, negotiating land purchases, and designing plans.

In 1899–1901, he built two eclectic apartment buildings with Art Nouveau elements, at no. 53–59 in Rue Victor Hugo in Schaerbeek. The façades combine polychromy with bricks and stone in various colours, and feature sgraffiti with inscriptions such as 'BE ACTIVE, BE CLEAN, SAVE, IN EVERYBODY'S INTEREST', in French and Dutch.

In 1903, the Foyer Schaerbeekois decided to raze two insalubrious alleys in the most densely populated part of the municipality, building a group of workers' houses, comprising five buildings. The two on the street side were similar and built on either side of a passage, through which a carriage could pass. The three other adjoining buildings were located at the other end of the courtyard.

The courtyard, which was planted with shrubs and plants, had a circular basin in the centre with a fountain, which is no longer there. As is the case for all the buildings in Rue Victor Hugo, the composition combines the polychromy of materials with sgraffiti by Privat Livemont.

Originally, each of the five-floor buildings had ten apartments, consisting of a kitchen, which also served as a living room, a laundry room, two bedrooms, a WC, and a terrace for plants. The tenants could use the flat roofs to dry their laundry.

The group of buildings, which was inaugurated on 16 July 1905, was an immediate success and there were numerous applications for apartments. The shop premises on the ground floor proved more difficult to rent because the rent was deemed too high. This was the first project of its kind and it inspired the design of Cité Hellemans in the Marolles, among others.

▼ Workers' houses, Rue L'Olivier 16–44

8/ HÔTEL COHN-DONNAY

RUE ROYALE 316, 1210 SAINT-JOSSE-TEN-NOODE

Architect: Paul Hamesse
1904
Listed: 8 August 1988

In 1904, the industrialist Cohn-Donnay tasked Paul Hamesse with the transformation and development of a building dating from 1841. He altered the neoclassical façade by adding a bay window in a more geometric style to it. The building's interior, however, is extraordinary and fortunately the decorations have been preserved. Inside, the architect combined different Art Nouveau trends, borrowing from the Glasgow School and the Viennese Secession while some motifs already pointed to the emergence of Art Deco.

The hallway floor is decorated with mosaics and the walls are painted with geometric patterns incorporating stylised figures of insects. A copper radiator cover, decorated with two pheasants facing one another, has been incorporated into a wooden coat rack with a mirror above it. The various radiator covers are of an exceptionally high standard. The hall leads into the former billiard room, which leads to a room for chess games.

On the side, the adjoining sitting rooms and the dining room, feature a series of decorations in different styles: neo-Greek for the sitting room on the street side, while the small central sitting room is influenced by Charles R. Mackintosh. The room's ceiling is decorated with flowers and a frieze featuring peacocks, which is repeated in the stained glass windows of the doors that lead into the billiard room.

At the rear, the garden no longer exists. The rock wall on one side of the garden has been preserved however, as has the passage that leads to the outbuildings. On the first floor, a room with columns and fluted pilasters with Ionic capitals extends along the façade. The marble fireplace is covered with a copper plate with a peacock motif, which was made by the same artisan as the radiator covers on the first floor.

At the rear the architect designed a poetry room, with a small dais in the corner, with a balustrade, for recitals.

For many years, the brasserie-restaurant De Ultieme Hallucinatie was located in Hôtel Cohn-Donnay. It recently reopened under a new name, The Ultimate Hallucination.

In Belgium, heritage conservation is a regional competence. In the Brussels-Capital Region, the Directorate of Monuments and Sites (DMS) is tasked with heritage **conservation and raising awareness about heritage**.

To carry out its mission, the administration has several legal instruments at its disposal, including:

- **the remarkable heritage inventory of the Brussels Region** (www.irismonument.be), which is available online and which is largely complete. This tool aims to draw the attention of owners and authorities to the heritage aspect of a property. Registering a property is not a protective measure. It only recognises the building's relevance;
- **permanent legal protection of heritage**:
  - **the grading** of a property ensures effective and rigorous protection, meaning any work the owner wishes to undertake is subject to planning permission. Some restoration work may eligible for a grant. A graded property is surrounded by a protected area, the scope of which is defined depending on the landscape or urban context. The protection zone aims to protect the perspectives that leads to and from a graded property;
  - **the listing of a building** is more flexible, making it easier to incorporate these listed properties into contemporary life. Planning permission may be given for the renovation of the building so it can be given a new designation. The heritage value of the property must always be guaranteed.

The Government, the Royal Commission for Monuments and Sites, the municipal authorities, and the owner or a heritage conservation association may all submit proposals for the listing of a building.

At the same time, the Directorate of Monuments and Sites pursues its efforts **to raise the public's awareness**, by organising its own projects and supporting private initiatives such as the Heritage Days, publications, brochures, exhibitions, conferences, and educational activities.

In 1999, the Directorate of Monuments and Sites took the initiative to establish the **Art Nouveau Network**, bringing together many organisations from European cities that also have a rich Art Nouveau heritage (Helsinki, Barcelona, Glasgow, Budapest, etc.), to study, preserve, and promote this heritage (www.artnouveau-net.eu).

▼ Chess room, Hôtel Cohn-Donnay
▼ Radiator cover, Hôtel Cohn-Donnay

GYMNASE

SEVENTH WALK

THE CENTRE OF SCHAERBEEK

From 1850 until 1900, the population of Schaerbeek increased from 8,630 to 64,000 inhabitants. The modest village was transformed into vast modern city. As a result, new neighbourhoods were developed where Art Nouveau found its place alongside the other styles that were popular at the time, mainly eclecticism. Throughout its history, the Municipality of Schaerbeek has supported urban and architectural projects with architectural competitions, awards for qualitative projects and, more recently, grants for qualitative renovations.

◂ Façade of the gym of the Josaphat School Group, 243, Rue Josaphat, Henri Jacobs, 1900-1907

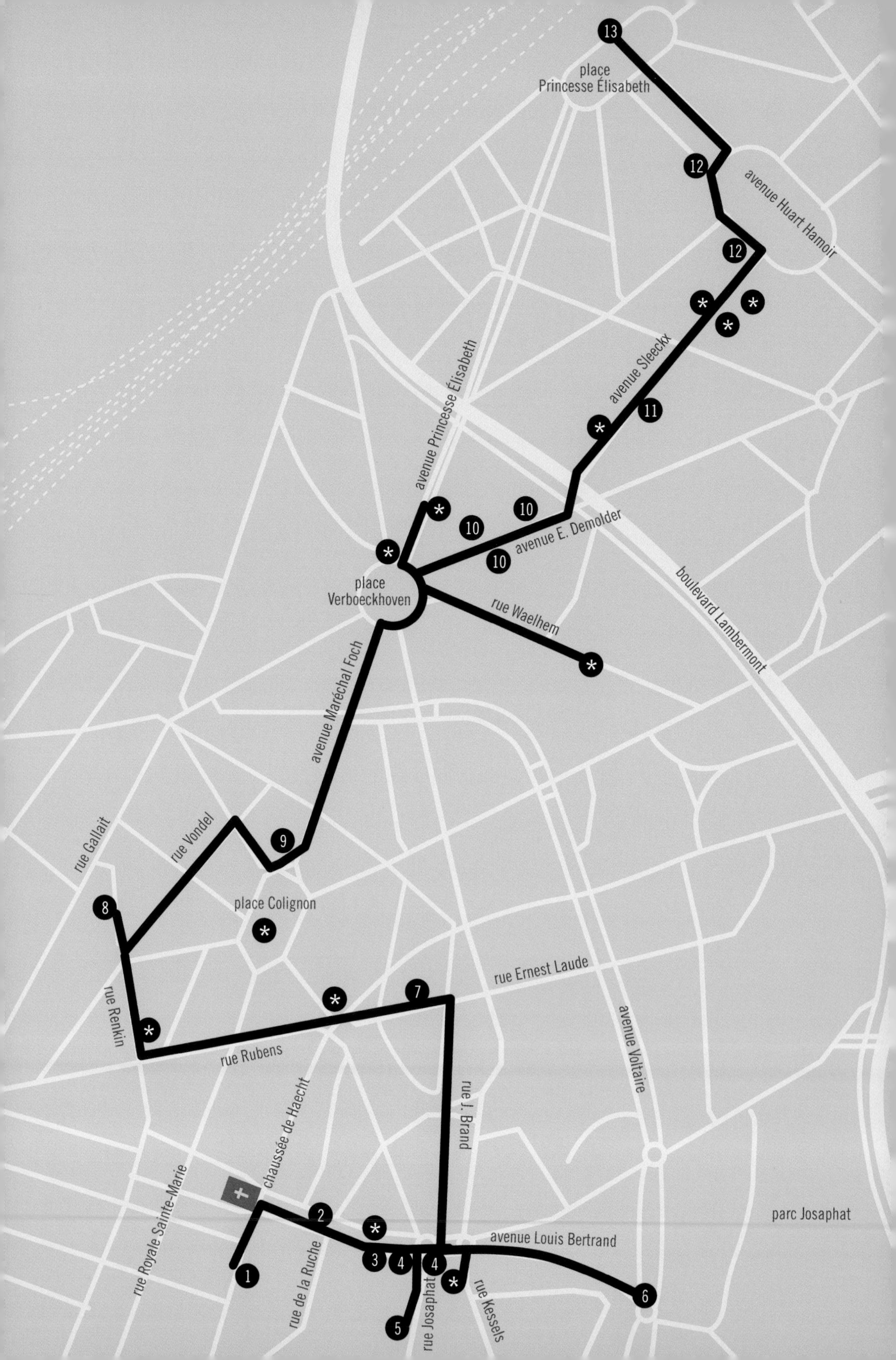
13
place
Princesse Élisabeth
12
avenue Huart Hamoir
12
avenue Sleeckx
11
avenue Princesse Élisabeth
10
10
10
avenue E. Demolder
place
Verboeckhoven
rue Waelhem
boulevard Lambermont
avenue Maréchal Foch
9
rue Vondel
rue Gallait
8
place Colignon
rue Ernest Laude
7
rue Renkin
rue Rubens
avenue Voltaire
chaussée de Haecht
rue J. Brand
rue Royale Sainte-Marie
2
3
4
4
avenue Louis Bertrand
parc Josaphat
1
rue de la Ruche
5
rue Josaphat
rue Kessels
6

01 **AUTRIQUE HOUSE**
CHAUSSÉE DE HAECHT 266, 1030 SCHAERBEEK

02 **AVENUE LOUIS BERTRAND**

03 **VERHAEGHE HOUSE**
AVENUE LOUIS BERTRAND 43, 1030 SCHAERBEEK

04 **APARTMENT BUILDINGS**
AVENUE LOUIS BERTRAND 53-61 AND 63-65
(CORNER OF RUE JOSAPHAT), 1030 SCHAERBEEK

05 **JOSAPHAT SCHOOL GROUP**
RUE JOSAPHAT 229, 1030 SCHAERBEEK

06 **ELECTRIC MAST *BATTLE BETWEEN TIGERS AND SERPENTS***
AVENUE PAUL DESCHANEL, 1030 SCHAERBEEK
(INTERSECTION WITH AV. LOUIS BERTRAND)

07 **DUPONT HOUSE**
RUE ERNEST LAUDE 20, 1030 SCHAERBEEK

08 **LANGBEHN HOUSE**
RUE RENKIN 90-92, 1030 SCHAERBEEK

09 **GROUP OF THREE HOUSES, INCLUDING THAT OF THE ARCHITECT HENRI JACOBS**
AVENUE MARÉCHAL FOCH 7–11, 1030 SCHAERBEEK

10 **AVENUE DEMOLDER**

11 **GROUP OF HOUSES**
AVENUE SLEECKX 34-44, 1030 SCHAERBEEK

12 **AVENUE HUART HAMOIR**

13 **SCHAERBEEK STATION AND TRAIN WORLD**
PLACE PRINCESSE ÉLISABETH 6, 1030 SCHAERBEEK

1/ AUTRIQUE HOUSE

CHAUSSÉE DE HAECHT 266, 1030 SCHAERBEEK

Architect: Victor Horta
1893
Listed: 30 March 1976

The engineer Eugène Autrique, whom Horta knew from the Masonic Lodge Les Amis Philanthropes, commissioned this house, which heralded the beginnings of Art Nouveau.

Horta succeeded in creating an original and inventive design with a limited budget. The construction of this house and, soon after, of Hôtel Tassel especially, marked a turning point in the young architect's career. The house was restored in 2002 and 2004 respectively by the architect Francis Metzger of Ma². François Schuiten and Benoît Peeters have since created an original scenography for it. It is now open to the public, and can be visited from the very top to the very bottom. As such, it evokes how people used to live in a late nineteenth-century Brussels residence.

The white stone façade, with red joints stands out from the adjoining façades, which are for the most part built in the neoclassical style. Horta was able to use white stone, which is more expensive than the plastered brick which Autrique could afford, because he agreed to charge only a modest fee for this project. He did, however, request to be reimbursed for his expenses.

The stone arch above the entrance door is slightly interrupted, a little reminder of neo-Gothic architecture. The façade has several air vents with elaborate bars in front of them. Originally there were supposed to be rooms in the attic but Horta chose to build a loggia instead, making the façade more expansive and original. In the centre, the wooden pillar that supports the protruding cornice rests on a carved stone column. The perimeter of the windows was decorated, which is rare in Horta's designs, with a bicoloured sgraffito with a linear whiplash motif.

Many of the façade's details refer to the owner's membership of the Masonic lodge, such as the triangle that constitutes the ironwork of the transom over the entrance door, the two ornamental elements that cap the façade and which are reminiscent of the falcon Horus.

There is nothing extravagant about this design, as Victor Horta stressed in his *Mémoires*: 'An inhabitable cellar, a vestibule and staircase that have merit, a pleasant combination of a dining room and sitting room, a first floor with bath and toilet (which was still a luxury at the time) and a second floor with attic rooms for the servants and children. Not exactly a palace for a king!'[1] Even though Horta still stuck to the traditional floor plan of Brussels houses, that is to say, three adjoining rooms, which are clearly separated from the stairwell, he added a series of structural and decorative innovations. On the upper floor, the four adjoining rooms—the smoking room, the sitting room, the dining room, and the winter garden—clearly belong together, although their decorative scheme, which remains eclectic, is different.

The metal lintels of the wooden coffered ceiling are visible, a characteristic of the style he was developing—Art Nouveau.

A marble mosaic, in white, red, and orange, with a sinuous motif, decorates the floor of the vestibule. The exotic wood of the flight of stairs also evokes the botanical world. Light enters the stairwell from above, thanks to stained glass windows on the mezzanine, with Japanese motifs.

2/ AVENUE LOUIS BERTRAND

Avenue Louis Bertrand was built in 1905, connecting the esplanade of Saint-Servais Church (Gustave Hansotte, 1871–1876) in Chaussée de Haecht, with Josaphat Park, which was built simultaneously. This tree-filled platform fans out as it extends towards the park, forming a large lawn. In view of this development, the old village centre of Schaerbeek was demolished.

The avenue pays tribute to Louis Bertrand (1856–1943), a key figure in the town planning and development of Schaerbeek, and an alderman from 1895 to 1920. Bertrand also founded the Belgian Workers Party, the newspaper Le Peuple and the Foyer Schaerbeekois public housing authority.

The surrounding area was built up before World War I, creating a particularly well-preserved group of upper middle class homes and apartment buildings, in the styles that were popular during the Belle Epoque: eclecticism, 'neo' styles and, of course, Art Nouveau. To ensure prestigious buildings would be built, the commune required that façades cost at least 50 francs per square metre and were at least six metres wide. The municipality would present awards to no fewer than twelve dwellings along the avenue, during the façade competitions it organised.

Midway, a bronze vase, by the sculptor Godefroid Devreese, stands in the middle of the avenue. It was presented to the commune by the industrialist Raoul Warocqué in 1911 and features a procession of satyrs and bacchantes, who accompany the god Bacchus.

▾ avenue Louis Bertrand before 1914

3/ VERHAEGHE HOUSE

AVENUE LOUIS BERTRAND 43, 1030 SCHAERBEEK

Architect: Gustave Strauven
1906
Listed: 13 July 2006

This façade, which has windows on almost every square metre, looks lively because of the sections that are set back and others that protrude from the façade: a bay window on the first floor, a loggia on the second, and a terrace on the uppermost floor. The entrance span features a turret and is particularly original: the entrance door is surmounted by a transom window with a stained-glass window; it also has windows in various shapes, and sills with sgraffiti.

The materials used here only serve to make the façade even livelier. Blue stone bands contrast with the enamelled white brick. The blue stone of the base is carved with floral reliefs, which feel slightly overdone. The elaborate ironwork and original woodwork have been retained.

Originally, a single-family dwelling (it is currently divided into apartments), the house has a traditional floor plan: the entrance hall and stairwell are to the right, while the bathrooms are located on the street side. The various living rooms are located to the left. The kitchens are in the cellar, the reception rooms on the upper floors and the bedrooms above them. Many of the original features of the interior decoration scheme have been retained.

At 38, Avenue Louis Bertrand, on the opposite side of the street, a geometric Art Nouveau house (Frans Hemelsoet, 1906), which received an award in the façades competition of 1907–1908, used to have sgraffito under the cornice.

4/ APARTMENT BUILDINGS

AVENUE LOUIS BERTRAND 53-61 AND 63-65 (CORNER OF RUE JOSAPHAT), 1030 SCHAERBEEK

Architect: Gustave Strauven

1906

Listed: 8 May 2008

The entrance in Josaphat Street is enhanced, in a masterful manner, by two groups of apartment buildings, built by Gustave Strauven with storefronts on the ground floor. These buildings are an excellent example of the architect's ingenuity: volumes protrude and are set back, he creates a polychrome façade by using bricks in different colours, masonry punctuated with blue stone bonds, ceramic decorations, cast iron balcony railings and columns, wood divisions for the windows and brackets that support the cornices.

Originally, the corner spans of the two buildings were both capped with a dome. That of the left building, at no. 63–65, has since disappeared. However, the building's striking wrought iron awning has been restored.

Two ceramic panels have been affixed above the architect's signature to the base of the right-hand building (no. 53–61), to the left of the door through which you enter to go to the apartments. One features a view of old Schaerbeek around the time of the first Saint-Servais church, which was demolished as part of the neighbourhood's development. The top panel represents a donkey's head surrounded by Morello cherries. These panels were produced by the Wezel ceramic factor, which was only a short walk away, in Rue Kessels. Schaerbeek used to be a rural hamlet, where vegetables were harvested, which were then brought to market. Seeing the donkeys, the people of Brussels used to exclaim: 'The Schaerbeek donkeys have arrived!', referring both to the animals and their owners. The tradition remained and Schaerbeek is still nicknamed the city of donkeys. There also used to be plenty of Morello cherry trees here. This tiny tart cherry is used to produce kriek, a spontaneous fermentation beer flavoured with cherry.

Nowadays the ground floor of both buildings is occupied by restaurants with an Art Nouveau feel to them.

▼ Ceramic panel, avenue Louis Bertrand 53-61

▼ Avenue Louis Bertrand 53-61

5/ JOSAPHAT SCHOOL GROUP

RUE JOSAPHAT 229, 1030 SCHAERBEEK

Architect: Henri Jacobs
1900-1907
Listed: 2 April 1999

▲ Main entrance of the primary school, Josaphat school group, Rue Josaphat 229.

This 'palatial school', which was solemnly inaugurated on 6 October 1907, was the pinnacle in Henri Jacobs's career. It sealed his reputation as an architect who could design anything on any type of land. There is not one, but two schools here, although they operate independently. The nursery and primary school can be accessed from Rue Josaphat, whereas the technical school and library can be reached from Rue de la Ruche. There are ninety-one rooms in all, and plenty of open space to accommodate up to 1,000 pupils—an exemplary model of organisation and equipment, as well as of heating, ventilation, and circulation!

The entrance in Rue Josaphat is monumental, but relatively narrow compared with the building's overall size. The façade combines blue stone, orange bricks, and white Euville stone, with sgraffiti with a stylised daisy motif. The blue stone frame around the central double oak door is capped with the torch of secularism, which is raised upwards and features cherry patterns on the pilasters. The façade also has a keystone, decorated with the Belgian heraldic lion.

At no. 243, Rue Josaphat, the gym's facade, made of white Euville stone on a blue stone base, has a large window, which rests on cast iron columns.

The interior is organised around a central double height courtyard, which opens out on either side onto a playground with large windows on two levels. The metal structure is visible and enhances the decoration. On the first floor, a gallery facilitates the children's circulation. Large panels with sgraffiti featuring stylised floral motifs frame women's faces and were the work of Privat Livemont.

The hall leads to the wings where the classrooms are located and is connected by a hallway to the gym and former swimming pool, which was closed in the Seventies. The construction of the swimming pool and forty showers was discussed on the town council. While physical education had become compulsory, many councillors deemed that a school swimming pool was excessive, especially given the fact that there was a public swimming pool nearby, which had been inaugurated in 1904 in Rue Kessels.

The tech school in Rue de la Ruche can be accessed by a long vestibule which leads to a ceremonial hall, followed by a large gallery that connects with the classrooms.

Henri Jacobs (1864–1935) studied at the Brussels Academy. After completing a few projects, mostly in Laeken, he was appointed in 1899 as the official architect of Foyer Schaerbeekois for whom he built innovative public housing projects, including a group of buildings in Rue Victor Hugo (1900) and Cité de l'Olivier (1905). Throughout his career, he also built private dwellings, including his own home, in Avenue Maréchal Foch in Schaerbeek.

He was one of the few Art Nouveau architects to focus on social housing and more specifically on school buildings. This is probably because his father was a former teacher, who had been promoted to the position of inspector in primary education facilities. Initially, he mainly built village schools in Flemish Brabant. Gradually he started to receive commissions from various Brussels municipalities, however, including Forest, Uccle, Brussels, Koekelberg, Auderghem, Etterbeek ... and Schaerbeek, of course, which has two striking groups of buildings by Jacobs: the Josaphat school group (1907) and the Linthout school group in Avenue de Roodebeek (1913–1922).

Since the mid-nineteenth century, a wind of change could clearly be felt in non-confessional education in Brussels. The construction, in 1875, of a model school (currently the Haute Ecole Francisco Ferrer) in Boulevard Lemonnier served as a reference for many of the schools that were subsequently built. The school is organised around a vast courtyard in the interior of the building block. The accent is primarily on hygiene (air and light) and physical education. Henri Jacobs followed this model in his building groups, creating Art Nouveau buildings and shapes and building gesamtkunstwerke. He combined a rational organisation with industrial materials, attention to detail, and refined decoration. Later on, the architect was often accused of creating a design that was too refined and too luxurious, but he considered this an integral part of this educational ideal: 'You can only encourage young pupils to love and respect what is good and beautiful by building something that is good and beautiful'.[2]

At 88, Rue Kessels, we pause to look at an Art Nouveau house that was built by François Hemelsoet in 1906. Its gable has a horseshoe-shaped window, with a small balcony that is connected to the terrace below with a metal column. This house has retained many of its original features, including some of the window frames, carved stone elements, some stunning wrought iron railings and a door that is signed by the craftsman Th. Marchal. The transom above the entrance door is decorated with a stained-glass window, depicting a swan that glides among the water lilies against the backdrop of a sunset.

The neighbouring house, no. 86, was built that same year by the same architect, but is more eclectic in style, although it does feature some Art Nouveau elements, including a stained-glass window in the transom.

6/ ELECTRIC MAST
BATTLE BETWEEN TIGERS AND SERPENTS
AVENUE PAUL DESCHANEL, 1030 SCHAERBEEK (INTERSECTION WITH AVENUE LOUIS BERTRAND)

Sculptor: Jacques de Lalaing
1887-1913
Listed: 4 June 2009

This Art Nouveau inspired bronze mast, which was designed between 1887 and 1913 by Jacques de Lalaing, was presented to the Municipality of Schaerbeek by his heirs in 1926. The town council decided to install it here. In 1953, the rather damaged mast was dismantled and stored in a warehouse after which it was reinstalled in Place Colignon, in front of the town hall in 1993. In 2006, it was moved again, to its original location, after which it was restored in 2012–2013.

A renowned portrait painter and sculptor, Jacques de Lalaing (1858–1917) excelled in the sculpture of wild animals and horses, his favourite themes. The Tiger Mast was the crowning masterpiece of his career. In 1887, he presented a first version of the mast, in plaster, which was a huge success. Afterwards, he tried to incorporate his work in public space, constantly remodelling it. He often travelled to the Antwerp Zoo to check whether he had the movements of the animals right, while working on the mast. The definitive version was presented at the World Expo in Ghent in 1913.

The mast's base features three high-reliefs, illustrating combat scenes between tigers and serpents, against a background of banana leaves. The mast, which is over fifteen metres high, has four lamps. The smooth movements of the tigers and the serpents that wind their bodies around the mast make the composition even more dynamic.

7/ DUPONT HOUSE
RUE ERNEST LAUDE 20, 1030 SCHAERBEEK
Architect: Joseph Diongre
1908

Joseph Diongre (1878–1963) is famous for his modernist houses, which he built in the decades between the two World Wars. They include the Church of Saint John the Baptist in Molenbeek (1930–1932), the National Broadcasting Institute (Institut National de la Radiodiffusion (1933–1939)) in Ixelles, and others. But prior to this, he worked in the eclectic and Art Nouveau styles. He lived in Schaerbeek before World War I, building several houses there, including his own, in Rue Léopold Courouble. From 1904 until 1924, he lectured in architecture at the Schaerbeek Industrial College. He built this house for one of his colleagues, the lawyer Georges Dupont, who lectured in economy.
The façade is eclectic but features some Art Nouveau elements, including sgraffiti by Privat Livemont. It won an award in the façades competition of 1908–1909.
Diongre and Livemont were colleagues at the Industrial College and worked together on several occasions.
The sgraffiti under the cornice represent ram's heads, holding garlands of daisies. Above the door, we see the profile of a young woman, with undulating locks. The colour of the sgraffiti blends in nicely with the red-orange brick façade, which is enlivened by a wood bay window, with a small stained glass window depicting a women in historical costume.

Privat Livemont (1861-1936) was a multitalented artist. He trained in Brussels, then moved to Paris, where he lived for seven years. He is mainly known for his work as a decorator, poster designer, and lithographer. He also created several murals. His career was inextricably linked with the Art Nouveau movement, working with several architects, including Henri Jacobs. Many of his works feature women. For Livemont, the woman's figure represents both a muse and an allegory. He takes great care tracing the woman's face and her curvaceous figure. Usually her eyes are closed, her hair is let down or contained in a messy bun. Livemont's work is often compared to that of the Czech poster designer Mucha, but should not be confused with it.

At no. 22 through to 26 in Rue Verwée, three Art Nouveau houses that were built by Henri Jacobs in 1903 are an excellent example of the architect's ingenuity. Although the houses were built on small parcels of land (less than 1.5 metres deep on the corner of the Chaussée de Haecht), Jacobs used a system of corbels on the upper floors, which allowed him to extend the houses by one metre. The houses had small stalls on the ground floor, and some of the shopfronts have been preserved.

The façades were originally decorated with sgraffiti and are punctuated with pilasters that evoke plant veins.

Before walking to Rue Renkin, after crossing Rue Royale Sainte-Marie, we owe it to ourselves to take a closer look at the town hall of Schaerbeek to our right. This Flemish neo-Renaissance work was inaugurated in 1887 (Jules Jacques Van Ysendyck).

At 33, Rue Renkin, the house of the architect Frans Van Ophem, which is built in an eclectic style, with picturesque tendencies, also features several Art Nouveau elements. The architect transformed a small building, which he used as a studio, into a prestigious residence for himself in 1903, incorporating his practice in it. The double façade stands out because of the variety of materials and how he used them. A wooden bay window, with a small balcony, creates a canopy over the entrance door. A frieze under the first-floor windows comprises eight sgraffiti depicting the construction trades.
In the left span, a relief by Victor De Haen represents a reclining young woman, in front of the dome of St Mary's Church.
Many of the original elements have been retained in the interior, especially in the hall and the stairwell, including the panelling, the stained glass, decorative paintings, and so on.

8/ LANGBEHN HOUSE

RUE RENKIN 90-92, 1030 SCHAERBEEK

Architect: Jean Van Hall
1901

The architect built this house for himself. Originally there was a small shop on the ground floor. It was occupied for many years by the mother of the artist Roger Langbehn, who died during the Battle of the Somme in 1918. The house has since been renovated and rebuilt and is now home to the Roger Langbehn Association for Education through the Arts and Respect for Nature (www.maisonlangbehn.be). The current owner was awarded the 2014 Heritage Prize of the Municipality of Schaerbeek for the quality of the restoration and the relevance of the house's new designation.

The façade is charming in every way because of the polychromy of the materials. The architect has used bricks in various colours, pink sandstone for the rubble on the ground floor, stained glass windows, and sgraffiti. There are references to nature everywhere. The ironwork of the cellar window, to the left, evokes a butterfly. The stained-glass windows, which are inspired by plants, were apparently created by Raphaël Evaldre. A dragonfly motif can be seen in the large window of the horseshoe-shaped arch on the upper floor. The sgraffiti with the floral motifs have been attributed to Adolphe Crespin. The main entrance door is surmounted by a wooden bay window, where the house's toilet was originally located.

9/ GROUP OF THREE HOUSES, INCLUDING THAT OF THE ARCHITECT HENRI JACOBS

AVENUE MARÉCHAL FOCH 7-11, 1030 SCHAERBEEK

Architect: Henri Jacobs
1905, 1899 and 1899
Listed: 12 September 1996

When he had to build a house for himself, Henri Jacobs obviously chose land in the commune where he worked most often. His personal home, in the centre of this group of houses, features a fan-shaped floral composition, which extends from the first floor and incorporates a large sgraffito by Privat Livemont. The sgraffiti of the sills on the ground floor surround the air vents, which feature the architect's monogram. The entrance door is protected by a small canopy, supported by stone consoles with an Art Nouveau profile. The decorative ironwork on the door, with its organic design, incorporates the letterbox, with the architect's name on it. The architect's practice occupied the upper floor, which had at least five desks, because Jacobs did not work alone. After his death, the house was transformed and divided into apartments. Jacobs built the adjoining house, to the right, at the same time as his own home, for a currency exchange agent. While it is similar in size, it is still very different: there are not that many sgraffiti on the façade, the uniform use of stone, neo-and Renaissance details. The metal sunshades partially cover the windows. Indoors, the rooms are arranged around a large vestibule and main wooden staircase. The house's stained-glass windows and sgraffiti have been retained.

In 1905, the municipal receiver, Vincent Coen, commissioned Henri Jacobs to build a house to the left of his own home for him. It won him the first prize in the façades competition of 1906–1907. Once again, the façade's composition shows how the architect paid attention to details. It is arranged around the main bay window, with its elegant metal structure, which has been decorated with sgraffiti by Privat Livemont. The bay window rests on two blue stone consoles. The one on the right serves as an extension of the mullion of the upper floor's bay window. The central mullion on the upper-most floor is flanked by a slender blue stone column that resembles a flower stem. The arched cornice features floral motifs.

The entrance door is surmounted by a transom window, with a stained-glass window with a floral motif. The metal door bell pull is still in place. The kitchen in the cellar was transformed into a garage in 1956. While the interior is rather eclectic in style, the sitting room and the dining room were decorated with canvases by Privat Livemont. At the rear, the house opens out onto the garden with a large veranda.

▲ Former depot of the de Palmboom brewery
▲ Home of Frans Hemelsoet

At 69–75, Rue Waelhem, the former warehouse of the Palmboom Brewery, in the eclectic style with Art Nouveau elements, was built in two phases, in 1907 and in 1913 (Florent Van Roelen). The complex is arranged a central courtyard and consists of warehouses, shops, stables, offices, and housing. The light brick façades are enlivened by red and orange brick bonds. The windows have various shapes, several of which are horseshoe-shaped. The arches of the windows and doors are punctuated by stone archivolts (contours) culminating in Art Nouveau scrolls. Various heavily damaged sgraffiti, featuring hop flowers, decorate the façades.

At 1–3, Avenue Princesse Élisabeth, on the corner of Place Verboekhoven, you will see an Art Nouveau apartment building by Frans Hemelsoet (1906). While the two domes that once stood on top of the small turrets on either side of the façade in the square, the building's striking large windows, which create a sense of unity between the ground floor and the mezzanine, have been retained.

At 22, Avenue Princesse Élisabeth, the façade of Frans Hemelsoet's own house, which was built in 1902 when the architect opened his own practice, combines Art Nouveau elements with the dominant neo-Renaissance style. The wrought-iron entrance door is especially original. It was originally decorated with stained glass and a door handle in the shape of a lizard. The office was on the ground floor, the reception rooms on the first floor and the bedrooms on the second. The stairwell has several Art Nouveau features, including a wrought iron railing and stained-glass windows. The reception rooms are in different styles, including neo-Renaissance and neo-Louis XVI. In his own house, the architect clearly demonstrates how he can reconcile the varied tastes of his bourgeois clientele. The house is currently divided into apartments.

10/ AVENUE DEMOLDER

The houses and small buildings in Avenue Demolder, much like those in Avenue Louis Bertrand, are typical of the upper middle classes' prevailing taste for a more eclectic style after World War I. After the zoning plans for the neighbourhood were approved in 1904, the first houses were built as early as 1907. Frans Hemelsoet built more than twenty houses here, making him the most represented architect in the neighbourhood. The houses are mainly eclectic in style, or were built in the Beaux-Arts style. Some have a small front garden. There are some examples of Art Nouveau here and there:

- at no. 24 (Frans Hemelsoet, 1907) the house's Art Nouveau ironwork railings are resplendent again. They were heavily damaged, dismantled, and restored in a workshop. Copies were made of the sections that were deemed too damaged and some were even in forged in the old style.
- no. 27 (Frans Hemelsoet, 1911), a Beaux-Arts house, was designed for a captain/commander in the artillery. It has floral sgraffiti, and the largest features a woman's face;
- nos. 42 and 44 were built in two phases for a businessman and have one façade. The twinned arched windows on the second floor, which are separated by a stem with a plant crown in the form of a slender column, are typical of the style of Henri Jacobs. No. 44, the part of the building to the right of the entrance door, was built in 1908. This town house has reception rooms on the ground floor, and bedrooms on the upper floors. The left span, or no. 42, which was built in 1911, consists of a small house above the carriage entrance.

▲ Avenue Demolder 24

At 31, Avenue Sleeckx, the Art Nouveau house of the architect Florent Rasquin (1911) has geometric sgraffiti, which were created by Paul Cauchie. The entrance has a stone awning, with prominent consoles and a sgraffito representing the architect's tools of the trade (compass and square). The sgraffito above represents a woman's profile surrounded by stylised flowers. The cellar light has bars with a geometric pattern. The stone arches, which are slightly broken, of the triple set of windows on the first floor only enhance the façade's original design.

11/ GROUP OF HOUSES

AVENUE SLEECKX 34-44, 1030 SCHAERBEEK

Architect: Frans Hemelsoet

▲ Avenue Sleeckx 42 et 44

This row of houses by Frans Hemelsoet (no. 42 has an error in the signature, E. Hemelsoet) shows how good the architect was at mixing styles.

Nos. 34 and 36 (1912) and nos. 38–40 (1912) are eclectic in style. No. 42 (1910) combines an eclectic style with Art Nouveau elements: the stone arch of the entrance door, the cornerstone of which reminds us of a very organic shell, the window frames of the windows (blue stone at the ends), which are sculpted with scrolls and foliage, and the ironwork railings with their stylised flowers.

The façade at no. 44 is clearly an Art Nouveau façade and looks more dynamic and organic than its neighbours as you can see from the rounded corners of the windows, the cast iron columns of the windows in the entrance span, the bay window that extends from the façade, the wrought iron grilles with their curved shapes, which were obviously inspired by natural forms. Above the windows on the upper floor and on either side of the curved cornice, carved stone elements in organic shapes enhance the verticality of the design.

At 76, Avenue Sleeckx, a recently-restored small Art Nouveau house (E. Van Lerberghe, 1910) has a wood bay window, with a terrace above it, which is protected by the overhanging cornice. Two floral sgraffiti by Privat Livement with women's profiles complete the decorative scheme.

At 69, Avenue Sleeckx, an eclectic house, which is clearly inspired by Art Nouveau (René Bartholeyns, 1911) is easy to recognise because of the prominent metal lintels. It has a vast mosaic at the top, representing two phoenixes against a plant backdrop.

At 90–92, Avenue Sleeckx, the Art Nouveau façade of a small apartment building, with a storefront and a carriage entrance (Frans Hemelsoet, 1912) is a combination of blue stone and red brick. The vertical rhythm is accentuated by vertical pilasters, the mullions of the windows, and the stone dividing elements of the balconies. The blue stone elements are sculpted with vegetal or geometric shapes.

François or Frans Hemelsoet (1875-1945) was born into a family of musicians. He studied at the Academy of Brussels in 1894 before continuing his training as an architect by designing houses, perhaps during an extended work placement with Henri Jacobs. In 1902, he opened his own practice. His output, which is beautifully finished, reflects the prevailing taste, from Rococo to the cottage style and Art Nouveau. He was a very popular architect with the upper middle classes. He was born in Schaerbeek and lived and worked there for the most part. He built several houses along the avenues that were developed in the early twentieth century, including in Avenue Demolder, along boulevard Lambermont and Avenue Princesse Élisabeth.

12/ AVENUE HUART HAMOIR

Avenue Huart Hamoir essentially is the neighbourhood's backbone. This tree-lined promenade extends from the Church of the Holy Family to Schaerbeek's station. Streets give out onto it, in an almost symmetrical manner. The avenue opened to traffic in 1908–1909. To the south, it is lined with eclectic buildings, which were for the most part built before World War I. The northern section of the avenue, as you move away from the centre of the municipality, was built during the Twenties and Thirties, and even later.

At no. 71, an eclectic house, which was clearly inspired by Art Nouveau (unknown architect, 1910) has a distinctive loggia with horseshoe-shaped arches on the upper floor. The triangular oriel in the entrance span is supported by a riveted metal console. The façade is decorated with a sgraffito with a woman's profile and stylised roses, which is signed Paul Cauchie. The top of the building, above the cornice, is rather unusual. To the left, a triangular wood dormer serves to extend the oriel. A stone dormer to the right has twinned window openings, one of which also has small balcony.

At no. 47–47a, an eclectic house with very discreet Art Nouveau references (Frantz Veldeman, 1915) has interesting stained glass windows inside, as well as some rather unusual ceramic decorations in the cellar. It is now a bed and breakfast (bnbbrussels.be/fr/chambres/633-1.html).

▲ Avenue Huart Hamoir 71

13/ SCHAERBEEK STATION AND TRAIN WORLD

PLACE PRINCESSE ÉLISABETH 6, 1030 SCHAERBEEK

Architect: Franz J. Seulen
1887 and 1913-1919
Listed: 10 November 1994

Clearly Schaerbeek Station, with its red brick and blue stone façades, bonds in Gobertange stone, and bulbous roofs does not qualify as an Art Nouveau building! This building is clearly inspired by the Flemish neo-Renaissance style and was built in two phases by Franz Seulen, the main architect of the Belgian National Railways. The oldest section (1887), to the left, was used for administrative purposes, with ticket counters, waiting rooms and offices. It also accommodated technical facilities and the house of the stationmaster. The modern part of the building (1913–1919) to the right is larger and more imposing. This had a large station hall and counters. The Art Nouveau influence is most apparent in this section, both on the outside and inside. The visible metal structure allowed the architect to add large windows, through which the light falls in, and create a vast station hall.
Schaerbeek Station is now home to Train World, the train museum. François Schuiten created the museum's surprising and dynamic scenography.

PORTRAIT: FRANÇOIS SCHUITEN

François Schuiten is a comic strip designer, who shot to fame with *Les Cités obscures*, a series he co-created with Benoît Peeters.

In it, he describes a parallel universe, in which architecture plays a crucial role. In 2002, he received the Grand Prix of the City of Angoulême for his entire body of work. But his universe extends beyond his drawing table and into Brussels, the city he calls home where, he lived in a house that was built by Frans Hemelsoet for many years. There he imagined the scenography of the Autrique House and of Train World.

Cécile Dubois: Bearing in mind the fact that your father, Robert Schuiten, was an architect, like your brother, do you think that your passion for architecture and all things urban runs in the family?

François Schuiten: I think there is definitely some truth in that. At the same time, my father was not exactly a conservationist, he did not defend heritage. He was a modern man[3], building quality houses for single households, whose urban projects were quite radical. In terms of urban planning, the utopian vision of the Sixties was quite fascinating... While this period is also responsible for a few calamities, I like the idea that people still believed that everything was possible, that the sky was the limit. Nowadays, we don't dream anymore. What I mainly remember from this era, is the vision, the desire to move forward, to build a new city that now no longer exists. I didn't inherit my preference for Art Nouveau as a style from my father. Perhaps it was my older brother Luc[4], or maybe the city itself inspired it. When you observe the city, you immediately become involved about the outcome of its story, about its heritage... Brussels makes you aware of architecture. You cannot ignore your responsibility when you look around at its buildings, at the city. Either it irritates you or makes you unhappy or you are passionate about it and amazed. Brussels is the kind of city that inspires this kind of sentiment.

CD: What gave you the idea for the scenography of the Autrique House?
FS: We started by looking at Brussels, and tried to understand what was missing and what constitutes the city's real charm. And ultimately, we realised that it is the fact that you can explore these traditional houses, that you can enter and feel their history, experience their roots... So we didn't want to create a new, traditional, expensive museum project. Instead we conceived a small and dynamic structure, similar to a laboratory, where everything is possible. We generally tend to standardise the relationship with heritage, but we can be much more creative... I would like people to be able to spend the night at the Autrique House. People like to enjoy a novel, somewhat surprising and astonishing experience...
We try to tell a story in the Autrique House and in Train World and people are genuinely interested in stories. They love to get caught up in them, they want to (re-)experience things.

CD: Do you have more ideas for Train World?
FS: I have so many dreams. I dream of opening the signal box to the public, which is really the most wonderful space. I want to create a railway garden along the tracks. I would love to see a centre open alongside Train World, which examines the mobility of the future. Brussels, which has so many mobility problems of its own, could take the lead and reflect on tomorrow's mobility. When faced with a desperate situation, you have two options. Either you can lament the situation, or you can start to rethink and rebuild everything.

CD: How did you become so passionate about trains?
FS: As a child, there was a railway near me, and I'd often see steam locomotives pass by. They were astoundingly beautiful. Designing a train is such a pleasure, especially the older type, which date from the time when Henry van de Velde was the artistic director of the Belgian National Railways. People had convictions back then, they had ambition. Nowadays, all they can talk about is profitability. The railways no longer inspire dreams. So how can we start dreaming about trains again? Train World offers us this option. It is a crucial project. Why? Because we need to revive the memory of that we used to be in his country. We must be proud again of the fact that at one time, this country was a pioneer in Europe, and the first with a railway! Train World is the kind of project that inspires pride and that is priceless, because pride has no price.

CD: What is your favourite Art Nouveau building in Brussels?
FS: I love them all and for different reasons. I love Hôtel Solvay a lot, because it is a "monster". It is not an easy house to live in. It has such an overwhelming presence, which verges on the asphyxiating. In that sense, I love it a lot as it represents a culminating point and because it tells a story, of a never-ending building project... After ten years, the Solvay family almost had to kick Horta out! What is so sad about Horta, is that they don't tell you what a fantastic architect he was. Most people think of him as a decorator. But Horta really was a revolutionary. He had his very own vision on space and light.

LEROY
6
H
H

EIGHTH WALK

THE SABLON AND MAROLLES NEIGHBOURHOODS

The Marolles neighbourhood is a very old neighbourhood. From the twelfth century onwards, a very active draper trade developed here. Whereas Rue Haute was lined with mansions and later with townhouses, the smaller streets and inner courtyards were built up with workers' houses. In the early nineteenth century, during the Industrial Revolution, the neighbourhood's population grew very quickly and the gardens of the old mansions were soon replaced with alleys, where a large working-class population accumulated. In the 1850s, the authorities undertook the remediation of the neighbourhood to deal with the issue of overcrowding, the risk of social conflict, and epidemics. They built Rue Blaes and Place du Jeu de Balle to solve the situation. In the twentieth century, many social housing complexes were built to get rid of the many insalubrious alleys.

◀ Galérie Leroy Frères – Lempertz 1845, Rue du Grand Cerf 6, Jules Barbier, 1900

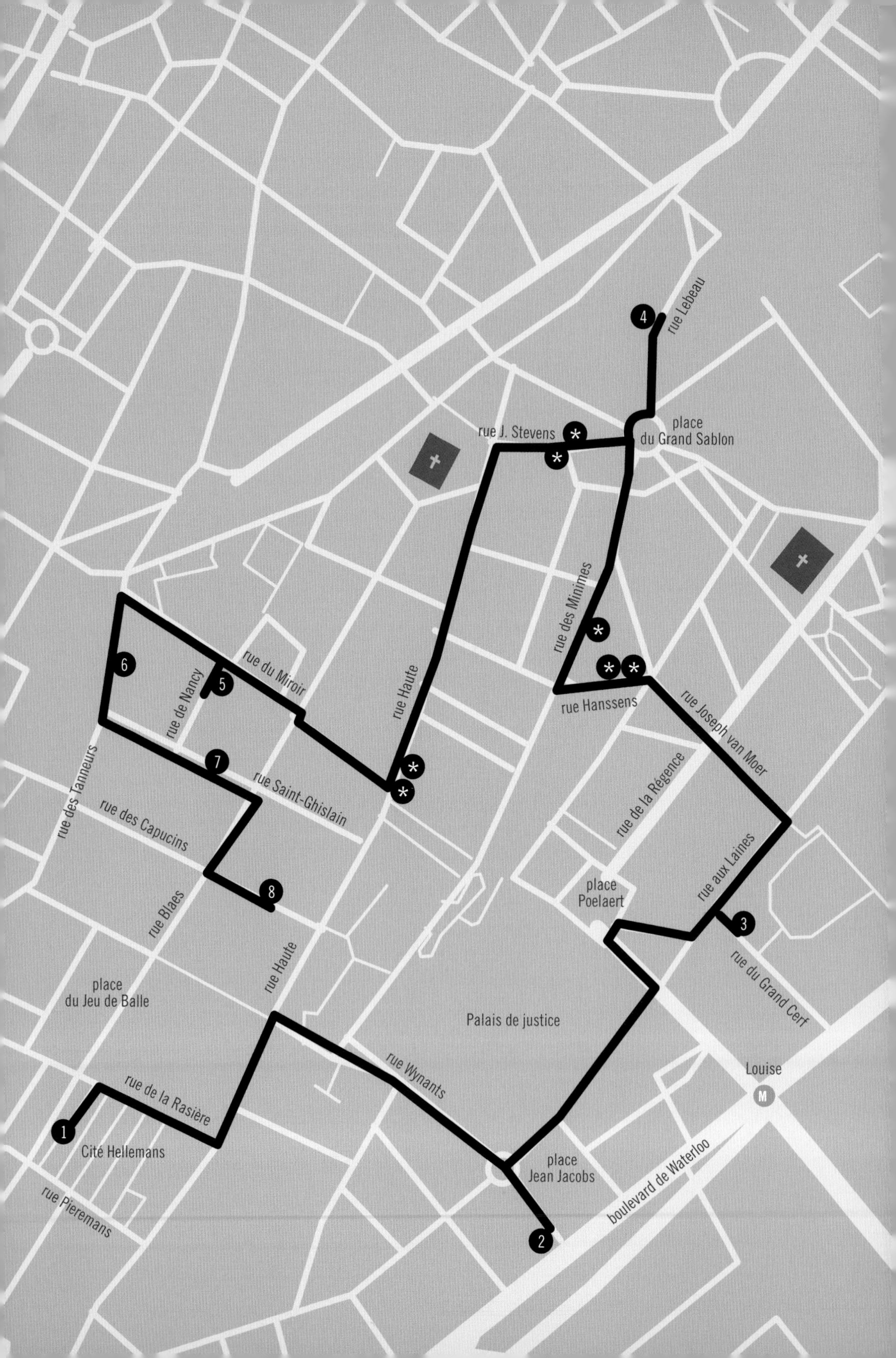

4
rue Lebeau
rue J. Stevens
place
du Grand Sablon
rue des Minimes
rue du Miroir
6
5
rue de Nancy
rue Haute
rue Hanssens
rue Joseph van Moer
7
rue Saint-Ghislain
rue des Tanneurs
rue des Capucins
rue de la Régence
rue aux Laines
8
place
Poelaert
3
rue Blaes
rue Haute
rue du Grand Cerf
place
du Jeu de Balle
Palais de justice
Louise
M
rue Wynants
rue de la Rasière
1
Cité Hellemans
place
Jean Jacobs
boulevard de Waterloo
rue Pieremans
2

01 **CITÉ HELLEMANS**
EXTENDING BETWEEN RUE HAUTE, RUE BLAES, RUE DE LA RASIÈRE AND RUE PIEREMANS, 1000 BRUSSELS

02 **PLACE JEAN JACOBS**

03 **GALERIE LEROY FRÈRES – LEMPERTZ 1845**
RUE DU GRAND CERF 6, 1000 BRUSSELS

04 **FRISON HOUSE**
RUE LEBEAU 37, 1000 BRUSSELS

05 **HOUSE AND STUDIO OF THE PAINTER CORTVRIENDT**
RUE DE NANCY 6-8, 1000 BRUSSELS

06 **PALAIS DU VIN**
RUE DES TANNEURS 58-62, 1000 BRUSSELS

07 **NURSERY SCHOOL**
RUE SAINT-GHISLAIN 40, 1000 BRUSSELS

08 **INSTITUT DIDEROT**
RUE DES CAPUCINS 58, 1000 BRUSSELS

1/ CITÉ HELLEMANS

EXTENDING BETWEEN RUE HAUTE, RUE BLAES, RUE DE LA RASIÈRE, AND RUE PIEREMANS

Architect: Émile Hellemans
1912–1917

This social housing complex, which was built by the City of Brussels, was devised from 1906 onwards. The project was finally undertaken in 1912 and the first tenants moved in as early as 1915. It replaced a network of alleys, with a population of over 2,000 people, who lived in insalubrious conditions and great misery.

The project reflects the hygienist ideas of the time. It features seven parallel housing blocks for several families and originally comprised 272 units, a nursery, and a laundry. The inner streets are connected by vaulted passages, which run under the buildings and which offer a beautiful central perspective.

The organisation of the building blocks shows how the designers strived to achieve hygiene, light, and social control!

Each unit has a living area, a certain number of rooms, a WC, its own water supply, a terrace, and a cellar which could be accessed from the courtyard.

The use of yellow, white, or red facing bricks, the metallic structure that was visible in several places, the rows of arcades, and a design that ensured that the light could reach the spaces—albeit not entirely successfully—in between the buildings all point to the Art Nouveau influence in this social housing project.

Today the complex is managed by Logement Bruxellois, a public real estate service. Cité Hellemans has since been renovated various times, to improve the comfort of the units. The façades and areas in and around the cité have also undergone alterations since then.

After focussing on various projects in his early career (mansions, castles, casino, a hospital, etc.) **Emile Hellemans (1853–1926)** turned his mind to housing for the poorest groups in society. As a member of the High Council for Public Hygiene, of the Patronage Committee for Workers' Housing, and the National Association Against Tuberculosis, Hellemans' efforts and work culminated in the construction of a complex that bears his name, heralding the increase in social housing after World War I.

2/ PLACE JEAN JACOBS

Place Jean Jacobs was built in 1890 to open a perspective from Boulevard de Waterloo towards the Law Courts, which were inaugurated in 1883. From the outset, the square attracted the bourgeois elite, which was seduced by its location, just a short walk to the prestigious Avenue Louise. The square is arranged around a public garden and has a row of striking houses, from no. 1 through to no. 17, on the south side. Their style varies from eclecticism to Art Nouveau (listed as a group on 27 May 1999).

Among this group, two Art Nouveau houses stand out from the rest.

No. 7, the lawyer Royer's house, was built in 1902 by the architect Georges Peereboom. It has a façade with a bell-shaped gable. The white stone façade rests on a red granite and blue stone base, with an oriel with a balcony and is definitely monumental in appearance. Its refinement, however, lies in the details: the entrance door is surmounted by a carved entablature and a wooden awning, which is supported by elegant consoles. The oriel's sill has been carved with flowering garlands, the sgraffiti, and the cast iron columns on the second floor, and the decorative anchors in wrought iron. The neighbouring house at no. 9, Dr Lebrun's home, was designed in 1903 by Georges Hobé and is less imposing. The façade is a mixture of blue stone for the base, and white stone combined with white brick. On the first floor, a triangular bay window in the centre of the façade rests on a console that extends from the base and which accentuates the balanced composition of the façade, which is symmetrical and was developed around a central axis. There is small balcony on top of the bay window, which was restored during a recent restoration. The narrow façade has a curved gable, with a hemispherical pediment and is flanked by graceful ornate fluted jambs that have been decorated with discs.

3/ GALERIE LEROY FRÈRES – LEMPERTZ 1845

RUE DU GRAND CERF 6, 1000 BRUSSELS

Architect: Jules Barbier
1900
Listed: 16 March 1995

This building has the same designation that it was originally built for. After restoration, it now is home to the Lempertz 1845 auction hall. In 1900, it was built for the Leroy brothers, who traded in paintings. At the rear, it has a vast rectangular showroom, with a glazed roof in a metal frame. The public can regularly visit the showroom. A door with bars in the façade, under the left window, gives access to the cellars, where the reserve is located. A lift, whose mechanism has been preserved, was used to transfer the works to the showroom.

The neo-Renaissance façade with Art Nouveau elements is polychrome because of the bricks in different colours and the recently restored sgraffiti, which list the names of the original owners and features the emblems of the arts (painting, music, sculpture, and architecture), which were produced by Adolphe Crespin.

The Art Nouveau approach is especially apparent in the architectural design for the left span: the metal lintel of the window on the upper floor, the sgraffiti, the cornice dormer, and the hipped roof.

The two neighbouring houses, at nos. 2 and 4 of Rue du Grand Cerf, including the house on the corner of Rue aux Laines, which is flanked by a small turret, dating from 1901–1902, were also designed by Jules Barbier in the neo-Flemish Renaissance style.

Jules Barbier (1865–1910), a former collaborator of Jules Jacques Van Ysendyck, who also worked on the design for the town hall of Schaerbeek, had an extensive working knowledge of historicist styles. In the early twentieth century, he also became interested in Art Nouveau. Most of his Art Nouveau projects were mainly located in Saint-Gilles and around the Cinquantenaire. Two works are important, the houses at nos. 5 and 6 in Avenue de l'Yser (Etterbeek), which are now listed.

At 31, Rue Watteeu, on the corner with Rue Charles Hanssens, an eclectic apartment building, dating from 1896, is home to an establishment on the ground floor, that has retained its Art Nouveau decorative scheme. Today it is occupied by the Le Perroquet Brewery.

At 9, Rue Charles Hanssens, a house in the eclectic style (Fernand Symons, 1896) features a set of sgraffiti, including a frieze with putti under the cornice. The next house, at no. 11, was built in 1899 and features ceramic polychrome panels in the spandrels of the entrance span, and is a more typical example of the Art Nouveau style.

At 40, Rue des Minimes, a neoclassical house that was built in 1897 has polychrome sgraffiti on the mezzanine level, which acted as a sign. Sunflowers, hence the inscription 'DE ZONNEBLOEM' (the Dutch word for sunflower) frame a woman's face.

4/ FRISON HOUSE

RUE LEBEAU 37, 1000 BRUSSELS

Architect: Victor Horta
1894
Listed: 21 April 1994

After building Maison Autrique and Hôtel Tassel, Victor Horta's career took off. In 1894, the lawyer Maurice Frison commissioned a building from him, combining his law firm with his home, to be built on a newly-created street. The design is as follows: the cellar is used for domestic activities. The law firm is on the ground floor, on the street side, the dining room and the veranda are on the garden side. The sitting rooms can be found on the first floor, while the bedrooms and bathroom are all located on the second floor. Light is drawn into the stairwell by a glass skylight.
The building was altered in 1954. The first floor office was relegated to the cellar and the windows were replaced with one single window, with a commercial entrance.
Take a few steps back to better appreciate the white stone façade with blue stone bonds, which features a curved balcony on the first floor with corner consoles and a slightly protruding bow window on the second floor, whose curve is similar to that of the balcony. The slightly overhanging window, which followed the line of the street, offers maximum light and lovely views. Unusually, the curved roof also has a large window so the attic rooms can be inhabited. The entrance is surmounted by a transom light with stained glass windows and ironwork.

The interior has retained some features of the architect's gesamtkunstwerk. The metal structure and stained glass window of the winter garden's skylight were restored in 1995 by Reuse and the glassmaker Jean-Marc Gdalewitch, under the supervision of architect-restorer Barbara Van der Wee. The original wall decorations, featuring arabesques, and which are particularly elaborate in the stairwell, were unearthed from under layers of paint and were restored.
In his *Mémoires* Horta writes that 'the design, including the expense incurred, was to everyone's satisfaction, including that of the client's fiancée'.[1] In 1899, Horta was asked to build a family house in the country in Avenue Circulaire in Uccle.

We exit the Sablon, and walk up Rue Joseph Stevens which is interrupted midway by a circular square, which has been dominated since the end of the 1960s (at 7, Rue Joseph Stevens) by a tower that will never be popular with the people of Brussels. This was where the Maison du Peuple once stood, which the Belgian Workers Party commissioned from Victor Horta in 1895. This imposing building, with its concave façade, and visible metal structure, offered various services to workers: there was a café and shops on the ground floor, offices on the upper floor and an events hall with exceptional acoustics that could accommodate up to 1,700 people on the uppermost floor. The Maison du Peuple was demolished in 1965, despite a petition from the Société Centrale d'Architecture de Belgique (SCAB). Instead it was tasked with dismantling certain parts of the building by the state.
All the buildings in the square have a concave façade, which is reminiscent of that of the Maison du Peuple. At no. 20, the former vocational school for carpentry (which now accommodates a section of the Institut Diderot), which was built in the Flemish neo-Renaissance style (Théo Serrure, 1895), has a polychrome façade with clearly visible metal elements, cast iron columns, and lintels. To the right, at no. 22, we see an Art Nouveau house (Paul Hermanus, 1903) with the original windows. The tympani of the windows on the second and third floor formerly featured sgraffiti.

We walk back to the Marolles. If you have the time, step inside the Easy Tempo restaurant at no. 146 Rue Haute. Here you can see the decorations of the former Pâtisserie de la Chapelle, which was built in 1918, when the building underwent transformations.
The storefront was replaced again in 1945. To the left, there is still a sales counter, while two panels on the right represent a pastry workshop and a tasting scene.
The ceramic tiles, used here for purposes of maintenance and hygiene, are often used to decorate the walls of shops, restaurants, tea rooms, and winter gardens during the Art Nouveau era. They often disappeared during alterations or renovations (the decorations were listed on 22 January 2004).

A little further up the road, at no. 158 Rue Haute, the building has retained its beautiful Art Nouveau shopfront (R. Neyberg, 1903–1904), with small transom windows with opalescent glass.

◂ Rue Joseph Stevens towards the Chapel Church. Left, Maison du Peuple, Victor Horta, 1895.

5/ HOUSE AND WORKSHOP OF THE PAINTER CORTVRIENDT

RUE DE NANCY 6-8, 1000 BRUSSELS

Architect: Léon Sneyers
1900
Listed: 29 January 1998

In 1900, the painter Albert Cortvriendt entrusted his friend the architect Léon Sneyers with the design of his home and studio. This was a great opportunity for the twenty-three-year old architect-decorator, allowing him to design a complete house, combining architecture and interior design. Sneyers, who had trained under Paul Hankar, here created a tribute to the master, who instigated the geometric trend in Art Nouveau.
The asymmetrical building, which is built on a shallow lot, is split into different parts. The house is on the left, and gives out onto a small courtyard. The vast studio is on the right, spanning the entire depth of the land. The floor plans of the two buildings have been combined in such a way that the rear part of the studio is significantly enlarged.
The white brick façade with red joints also features white and blue stone elements. To the left, we see a bay window surmounted by a balcony that is protected by the overhanging cornice as well as two other balconies to the right, which add a sense of relief to the façade.
In 2004, a restoration campaign focused on the façades and interiors. All the joinery was restored and stained glass windows added to the doors, which were recreated by the glass artist Jean-Marc Gdalewitch, and the sgraffiti restored to their former brilliance.
The geometric inspiration is particularly apparent in the sgraffiti, the stained glass, the wrought iron elements, the blue stone elements, and the woodwork.

The sgraffito panels and the geometric floral arrangements are attributed to Adolphe Crespin, under whom Leon Sneyers also trained and who produced most of the sgraffiti for Paul Hankar's buildings.

▲ Entrance door to the house of painter Cortvriendt

The interiors were renovated over the years. Today the two entities have been separated again and are now rented out separately by the public social welfare centre of the City of Brussels, which owns the buildings.

The entrance door to the workshop is a perfect expression of the architect's talent. Its blue stone door jambs feature two round copper plaques, that refer to the building's first owner. Coloured light falls into the hall through the two small stained glass windows in the window openings. A lovely copper feature is used as a letterbox, door handle and peephole.

Léon Sneyers (1877-1949) is primarily known as a decorator. His architectural work is less known. He played a vital role in the dissemination of the Viennese style in Belgium. He trained under Paul Hankar, working for him from 1897 until 1900 but also took classes with his colleague and friend Adolphe Crespin at the Academy of Fine Arts of Brussels. After Hankar's death in 1901, Sneyers and Crespin joined forces. They designed a studio as a tribute to Paul Hankar for the first Exhibition of modern decorative art in Turin in 1902, which was critically acclaimed. After this, Sneyers started to specialise in exhibition pavilions. He also discovered the creations of the Viennese Secessionists in Turin, which would heavily influence his work, and the construction, in Brussels, of the Stoclet Palace (1905-1911). He stopped using natural motifs, focusing instead on the combination of interconnected spaces and volumes. In 1906, he opened L'Intérieur, a gallery in rue de Namur, where he exhibited his own output and that of international creators, including the artists of the Viennese Secession. The gallery closed in 1918 and reopened as Galerie Sneyers in boulevard de Waterloo.

6/ PALAIS DU VIN

RUE DES TANNEURS 58-62, 1000 BRUSSELS

Architect: Ferdinand Symons
1909
Listed: 29 March 2001

In 1909, the Brias-Catteau company, a wine merchant that had established a presence in the neighbourhood since 1892, underwent a radical transformation, tasking the architect Fernand Symons with the reconstruction of its warehouses in the Art Nouveau style. The long polychrome façade of the Palais du Vin is composed of fifteen similar spans, each comprising two tiers of windows, surmounted with a curved tympanum that has been decorated with a sgraffito, protected by a border with an interrupted arch.
These sgraffiti, which are the work of Géo Ponchon, refer to famous wine regions, with various coats of arms of cities and regions, including Porto, Bordeaux, Madeira, Malaga, and Burgundy. The façade is surmounted by a railing with metal plates and a monumental curved pediment, which is off centre. The windows let the light fall into the cask hall, which is currently home to a restaurant called La Cantine. The vine and the grapes are still echoed in the wrought iron bars of the entrance doors and in the keystone in the pediment.
The warehouse, which was mostly built in reinforced concrete, with masonry, comprises two halls, which are separated by offices and services, which are later replaced with wine barrels.
Palais du Vin is a fine example of early twentieth-century architecture. The Brussels public social welfare centre acquired the building in 1996, as well as the old Merchie-Pède department store. The building underwent a thorough restoration and is now home to the Ateliers des Tanneurs, a business centre which also hosts events.

During his career, **Fernand Symons (1869–1942)** developed various types of designs, combining the eclectic style with Art Nouveau elements in a very upbeat manner. Palais du Vin was his first industrial building. Besides several residential houses, Symons also built two school buildings in Brussels, testifying to his pragmatic approach to Hygiene and Construction: Kindergarten no. 4 at Rue de Locquenghien in Brussels (1903–1908), and the nursery of Nid, Rue du Nid in Ixelles (1911). His achievements are characterised by the polychrome of the materials, but also by the frequent association of sgraffiti, often created by Géo Ponchon.

7/ NURSERY SCHOOL

RUE SAINT-GHISLAIN 40, 1000 BRUSSELS

Architect: Victor Horta
1895
Listed: 30 March 1976

As recounted by Victor Horta in his *Mémoires*, shortly after the construction of the Frison house, 'Buls, the Mayor of Brussels, happened to be passing by and finding the building to his liking, sent for me to his office: 'I saw your office, I'm interested in it. Do you want to create the design for a nursery school in Rue Saint-Ghislain for my administration? Did I want to? Of course!'[2] And that is how Victor Horta embarked on this unusual adventure. The school was completed in 1900 and originally could only accommodate 200 children.

The façade consists of a central section, where the entrance is located, as well as the concierge's office and the office of the head teacher. The two lateral wings, with one floor each, have large windows, containing one class each. The windows of the right wings are surmounted by a mosaic frieze bearing the inscription 'nursery school' in two languages.

The façade combines blue stone, Euville stone and stone from Gobertange, which were all used in a very refined manner.

The architect got into seriously hot water with the contractor, who found the stone carving work too difficult. As the shape of the stonework was quite complex, Victor Horta's workshop was asked to supply plaster models to the stone-cutters, which significantly slowed down the building process.

The main span in particular attracts the attention. On the left corner, two chimney flues are grouped, forming a tiny niche.

The right part is designed as a turret with a bell tower, with vertical stone mouldings that extend into flowers accentuating the building's height. This small turret also contains the stairwell. In the centre, the entrance door, which was made especially attractive for small children, is protected by an awning. Its carved consoles fan out towards the exterior, like two open arms, preparing for an embrace. The interior is organised around a covered courtyard with a light metal frame that incorporates a skylight that lets in a lot of light. The lower part of the walls is covered with white sandstone tiles, resting on a blue stone base. The four classrooms open out at the corners, two on the street side and two to rear, and have been symmetrically arranged. Two small courtyards fit between the classrooms at the front and back, offering the children a more intimate space to play. They used to be heated. In the outside playground, screens protect the entrance to the washrooms. In 1999, Barbara Van der Wee renovated the nursery school.

8/ INSTITUT DIDEROT

RUE DES CAPUCINS 58, 1000 BRUSSELS

Architect: Henri Jacobs
1902-1911
Listed: 19 February 1998

▲ Sgraffito in the playground of Institut Diderot

After the Josaphat school group in Schaerbeek, Henri Jacobs, the architect who designed Art Nouveau school buildings, was tasked with the design of the École Normale Émile André, the current Diderot Institute, which was inaugurated on 6 November 1910.

The narrow and discreet façade on the street side reveals nothing about the building concealed behind it. The entrance leads into a large covered courtyard, arranged width-wise, in a courtyard, with three perpendicular wings around it, where the classrooms are located as well as the gym. They are separated by playgrounds, which provide the children with light and air. Once again, Jacobs thought about the building's functionality first and foremost, while also paying attention to the decoration. He designed almost everything, including wrought iron railings, lighting, and the mouldings of the ceilings. The interior is decorated with a sgraffito by Privat Livemont, including a large panel representing the Archangel Michael, the patron saint of Brussels, who defeats the dragon against a landscape background, in which we can make out the law courts and the Brussels town hall.

INDUSTRIE

NINTH WALK

THE CENTRE OF BRUSSELS

This visit of the city centre allows you to discover the diversity of the Art Nouveau designs in this part of the city, often among much older buildings. The trail includes department stores, office buildings, apartment buildings, and events hall.

◂ Ceramic panel at Grande Maison de Blanc, Rue du Marché aux Poulets 32–34, Privat Livemont, 1896–1897

rue du Marais
rue Saint-Laurent
boulevard Pacheco
rue des Sables
rue Royale
rue des Comédiens
rue M. aux Herbes Potagères
rue de l'Écuyer
rue des Fripiers
boulevard Anspach
rue du M. aux Poulets
Bourse
rue d'Arenberg
Galeries Royales
rue de la Presse
place de Louvain
rue de Louvain
Parc
rue de la Loi
Grand-Place
rue du Midi
rue des Teinturiers
rue de l'Étuve
rue des Éperonniers
rue de la Madeleine
Gare Centrale
rue du Lombard
boulevard de l'Empereur
rue Ravenstein
parc royal
rue Ducale
Arts-
Mont des Arts
place Royale
rue de la Régence
1
2
3
4
5
6
7
8

01 **CHANCELLERY OF THE FRENCH EMBASSY**
RUE DUCALE 65, 1000 BRUSSELS

02 **WAUCQUEZ DEPARTMENT STORE – BELGIAN COMIC STRIP CENTRERUE**
RUE DES SABLES 20, 1000 BRUSSELS

03 **WOLFERS DEPARTMENT STORE**
RUE D'ARENBERG 11-13, 1000 BRUSSELS

04 **GRANDE MAISON DE BLANC**
RUE DU MARCHÉ AUX POULETS 32-34, 1000 BRUSSELS

05 **CINÉMA PATHÉ PALACE**
BOULEVARD ANSPACH 85, 1000 BRUSSELS

06 **COMMEMORATIVE PLAQUE FOR CHARLES BULS**
CORNER OF GRAND-PLACE AND RUE CHARLES BULS

07 **OLD ENGLAND DEPARTMENT STORE – MUSICAL INSTRUMENTS MUSEUM (MIM)**
RUE MONTAGNE DE LA COUR 2, 1000 BRUSSELS

08 **HÔTEL GRESHAM AND MUSEUM FIN-DE-SIÈCLE MUSEUM**
PLACE ROYALE 3, 1000 BRUSSELS

1/ CHANCELLERY OF THE FRENCH EMBASSY
RUE DUCALE 65, 1000 BRUSSELS
Architect: Georges Chedanne
1910-1911
Listed: 17 June 2010

This building is a unique example of French Art Nouveau in Brussels! Furthermore, its designation hasn't changed since it was built.

In 1910, the French Ministry of Foreign Affairs entrusted the architect Georges Chedanne with the commission to design the embassy's chancellery in Belgium, close to Belgian institutions.

Georges Chedanne (1861–1940), a French architect who studied at the Ecole des Beaux-Arts in Paris and won the Grand Prix de Rome in 1887, had just completed the French Embassy in Vienna (1901–1909) and the French legation in Beijing (1905). He was an established architect. He designed several buildings in Paris, in his own personal version of the eclectic style, with Art Nouveau influences. He built the Galéries Lafayette for example (1908).

The façade's balanced composition is tributary to the Paris School of Art Nouveau. The white stone façade has two floors and is divided into three separate spans of equal width by pilasters. The double leaves of the central door feature exceptional wrought ironwork, consisting of plant motifs, including pine cones that highlight the golden initials of the French Republic. On the upper floor, each span has three twin windows, surrounded by an oak leaf decoration on either side of the inscription 'R.F.' for French Republic. Under the curvy windowsills, we can distinguish a frieze of foliage and consoles caved with allegorical figures that embody the republic's motto of 'Freedom, Equality, and Fraternity'.

The Perret Brothers' company ,which specialised in reinforced concrete structures, built the chancellery. The French joiner Tony Selmersheim (1871–1971) was in charge of the woodwork.

As for the ironwork, it may have been sourced from the workshops of Louis Majorelle, one of the masters of the School of Nancy with whom Chedanne collaborated on several occasions.

The interior retained most of its original decorations, as well as some pieces of furniture.

At 13, Rue Royale, during the opening hours of the florist Daniel Ost, you can see the window display of the old Niguet shirt shop, built in 1896 by Paul Hankar (listed 17 February 2011). This window display is almost entirely glazed and features a floral decoration with small divisions. The main entrance is slightly set back. After the restoration in 2003–2004, the interior's original decorative scheme was restored, including a ceiling by Adolphe Crespin.

2/ MAGASINS WAUCQUEZ - MUSÉE DE LA BD

RUE DES SABLES 20, 1000 BRUSSELS

Architect: Victor Horta
1905-1906
Listed: 16 October 1975

The fabric merchant Charles Waucquez moved into what was essentially a very dynamic neighbourhood at the time, in the early twentieth century. The Waucquez Department Store sold draperies for men and new items for women, and dispatched supplies to all over the country. Victor Horta's design perfectly matched the client's requirements, who required large storage spaces, offices, and displays with plenty of light. The white Euville stone façade has large windows. The metal structure is not visible as Horta's style had been toned down somewhat by then. Not a single detail is left to chance; however, as you can see in the rounded angled of the windows, the refined design of the bars on the ground floor windows, the windowsills on the upper floor have triple air vents, recalling the division of the window frames.

Once you step through the central door and into the monumental corridor, you enter a monumental open space, that bathes in light from the skylight above. The building's metal structure is very visible. A monumental electric luminaire stands in the centre of the space, on a pink granite base, consisting of a metallic structure with five glass globes. Behind the iron and glass walls, visitor could just make out the storage rooms in the shadows, before walking up the monumental staircase, where they could take a closer look at the fabrics, under the natural light of the skylight.

The building was vacated in 1971 and suffered for many years, despite being listed as early as 1975. Heritage and comics fans finally came up with the idea of establishing a comic strip museum. In 1893, the Ministry of Public Works acquired the building, which reopened as a museum after restoration on 6 October 1989.

During his career, Victor Horta was asked to create several designs for large department stores. His metal structures were perfectly suited for the construction of large complexes lit by skylights. His most famous achievement was the Innovation, in Rue Neuve, which was inaugurated in 1903. As usual, Horta did not just design the architecture, but also created all the oak furniture, the hanging lanterns, the illuminated advertising, and so on. The owners, who were very satisfied, then entrusted Horta with the construction of their shops in Ixelles (1903) and Antwerp (1906) and hired him, after World War I, as a technical advisor.

Unfortunately, the store on Rue Neuve was destroyed by fire on 22 May 1967. Of all the department stores that Horta built, only the Waucquez store has been preserved.

At 33–35, Rue des Sables you can find the former headquarters of the newspaper *Le Peuple*, which is used today as part of the Comic Strip Centre, after several years of abandonment and a restoration. In 1905, Richard Pringiers (1869–1937), a former collaborator of Victor Horta and the architect of the Belgian Workers Party (POB), designed the headquarters of this socialist daily, which was founded in 1885 (listed on 12 June 2003). The Art Nouveau style of this building in blue stone and red brick is very simple. The ground floor was radically transformed in 1931, in the functionalist style, by Fernand and Maxime Brunfaut. The extension at no. 36–38 in Rue Saint-Laurent was built around the same time. The building is almost entirely glazed, and has a standard tower.

3/ MAGASINS WOLFERS

RUE D'ARENBERG 11-13, 1000 BRUSSELS

Architect: Victor Horta
1909-1912
Listed: 1 October 1981

In 1909, Victor Horta received a commission to design the stores and workshops of the Wolfers Brothers. This family of goldsmiths of German origin had been based in Brussels since 1812. In the early twentieth century, the company was managed by three family members: Philippe (1858–1929), the artist, who trained as a goldsmith, but also worked as a sculptor; Max (1856–1953), the elder brother, who specialised in sales and purchases; and Albert (1863–1930), the cousin and brother-in-law, who was responsible for the accounts.
'They complement each other so completely that you could say that they are three heads under a single cap',[1] Horta wrote. At the turn of the nineteenth and twentieth centuries, the company strengthened its reputation thanks to the creations of Philippe, whose Art Nouveau jewels were simply breathtaking.
Victor Horta was a longstanding acquaintance of the family. He was excited about the commission, even though the chosen site was inconvenient and Philippe Wolfers got it into this head that he wanted to give the architect guidance: '[I] have always hated busybodies. I have always hated those who are at good at something and imagine that they know everything about something else, that is not their job, feeling that they could do a better job than those who have spent their entire life studying this.'[2]The design was complex because it had to include 'shops, showrooms, a factory,

a jewellery workshop, sculpture workshops, storefronts for rent on the street side, and private floors, which could serve as a summer pied-à-terre and housing for workers.'[3] Horta arranged all this in a very practical way to minimise the loss of time and money. He chose to organise everything around a central courtyard, but Philippe Wolfers opposed the idea, demanding that two courtyards be built against the adjoining walls. Horta gave in, in everybody's interest... The main façade highlights the prestigious materials Horta used, worthy of the company's reputation. On the ground floor level, finely chiselled black granite was used to enhance the window displays. The first two levels were intended for offices, while the top floor, which is designed as a loggia, houses the director's apartment. As was the case in the Waucquez department store, the façade metal structure is no longer visible. It appears elsewhere, however, in the courtyards, and is especially complex, varying on each floor. The shop's furniture, in mahogany and drawn by the master himself, was bequeathed by the Wolfers family to the Royal Museums of Art and History upon the sale of the building in 1974 to a bank that still occupies the premises. The retail space was transformed. The Carrara marble staircase in the entrance axis, with its glass skylight, was preserved. This originally led to the first mezzanine where the showroom was located.

Step through the door of Restaurant Vincent at number 8-10 in Rue des Dominicains. The front of house and the open kitchen feature an extraordinary ceramic decoration on the walls and ceilings. This was produced in 1913 by Helman's workshops in Berchem-Sainte-Agathe, one of the leading Belgian manufacturers of ceramic decorations. The large paintings depict typical scenes of the Belgian coast and polders: fishermen shrimping on horseback, a fishing boat taking to sea, flying ducks over the polders, and cows and sheep in the grass. The ensemble is supplemented with ceramics with stylised geometric patterns that are very similar to Art Nouveau in style (listed on 20 September 2001).

At 47, Rue de l'Écuyer you can see an apartment building that was built in 1907–1908 by Paul Hamesse in a geometric Art Nouveau style (listed on 26 January 1995).

4/ GRANDE MAISON DE BLANC

RUE DU MARCHÉ AUX POULETS 32-34, 1000 BRUSSELS

Architect: Oscar François
1896-1897
Listed: 24 January 1991

Founded in 1864, the Grande Maison de Blanc commissioned buildings in the eclectic style in 1897 (Oscar François). This store, which was also a supplier to the Royal Court, sold all the textile products an upper middle class family might need for the house including tablecloths, curtains, bedspreads, fabrics, clothing fabrics, lingerie, and lace. The ceramic panels on the façade illustrate the variety of products on sale and were produced by Boch Frères Keramis of La Louvière, after cartoons by Privat Livemont. Young women are represented in profile, with messy hair with a flower

wearing loose and light dresses, with ribbons and silk threads and plenty of arabesques.
The influence of Japonism is felt both at the level of the thicker line that defines the drawings and delimits the large areas of colour (which suggests the sgraffito technique on the visual level) and the flowering cherry tree branches. Two female figures, wearing winged helmets and a heavy coat, face us, in a more solemn position. They are the allegories of commerce and industry. The ceramic decorations of the uppermost floor, which are less refined, are not by Privat Livemont. While the retail premises on the ground floor have been irremediably disfigured, the upper floors were restored to their former splendour in the early 2000s. An Art Nouveau storefront of such a size is particularly valuable: only a few have survived, given the transformations that these shops regularly undergo. Thanks to the opportunities offered by ceramics, the façade's decoration masterfully illustrates the building's function.

At the end of the nineteenth century, when Art Nouveau flourished, a **modern ceramic tile production industry** developed in Belgium. Tiles covered façades and the walls of vestibules, kitchens, bathrooms, toilets, shops, restaurants, winter gardens, and so on; they were sometimes white, sometimes coloured, and even decorated with relief patterns. In some cases, they were even used to create entire decorative panels. They were easy to maintain, withstood the test of time, and were also hygienic. Furthermore, you could combine colours and whimsical patterns with architecture.

▲ Ceramic panel, Avenue Louis Bertrand 53–61, 1030 Schaerbeek

Their production and use continued to be quite expensive however until after World War I. That is why you will mostly find these tiles in upper middle class homes or in buildings with very specific design requirements, where tiles added value, whether on the hygienic or commercial level. The tile manufacturers worked with their own workshops but also with external creators, including architects, painters, and poster designers. The majority of all Art Nouveau ceramic decorations in Brussels were produced by three factories: Célestin Helman's factory in Berchem-Sainte-Agathe, the smaller and more artisanal factory of Guillaume Janssens, also in Berchem-Sainte-Agathe, and the Vermeren-Coché porcelain factory in Ixelles.

On both sides of Stock Exchange, which was inaugurated in 1873 (Léon Suys), two establishments recall the splendour of the cafés along the boulevards during La Belle Epoque, combining comfort with lavish decorations, including panelling, mirrors that enlarged the space, and benches along the walls.
Cirio, at 18–20 Rue de la Bourse, was redecorated in 1909 by the decorator Henri Coosemans (listed on 3 March 2011). Everything here has been preserved, except the counter, which lists 1886 as a date. The café is named after its founder, Francesco Cirio, an Italian businessman who ran a food company in Turin, which opened several tea rooms across Europe. The Brussels branch is the only one still in existence. The successive owners have all chosen to retain the café's name.
Falstaff, at 17–19 Rue Henri Maus, was built in various phases between 1903 and 1916 by the decorator Émile Houbion, and still has a splendid Art Nouveau storefront, combined with an Art Deco sign from 1930 (listed on 12 October 2000). The interior decoration is lavish, with panelling and mirrors, large windows decorated with stained glass, chandeliers and bronze wall sconces, period furniture...

5/ CINÉMA PATHÉ PALACE

BOULEVARD ANSPACH 85, 1000 BRUSSELS

Architect: Paul Hamesse
1913
Listed: 27 March 1997

In the early twentieth century, cinema was considered a popular and immoral pastime—a silly form of entertainment, without any artistic future! The construction of the Pathé Palace for Les Grands Palais d'Attraction Pathé Frères in 1913 marked a turning point. This was the first ever cinema in Brussels, which could seat 2,500 film fans. It was intended for a bourgeois clientele and had to rival the prestigious theatres in the capital in terms of comfort.

The design features a large projection room, with an eclectic decoration, capped with a dome, with an orchestra pit (remember, this was the era of silent movies) and a stage for music hall skits. It also had a foyer in the geometric Art Nouveau style, a winter garden, and a restaurant. In this project, the architect Paul Hamesse combined everything his two masters had taught him. Alban Chambon, who specialised in the design of entertainment venues and Paul Hankar, who instructed him in the geometric Art Nouveau style, which was later enhanced by additions from the Viennese Secession.

In 1950, the building was radically altered. It ceased to operate as a cinema in 1973. It was subsequently used as the retail premises of a large appliance store. In 1999, the Palace became a cinema again for a brief time and was renamed Kladaradatsch (Yiddish for 'big spectacle'). In 2003, the French-speaking Community acquired the building and commenced its restoration, which is still ongoing. Paul Hamesse's architecture will be restored to its former splendour in the long term. The dome of the old cinema and the foyer above the main entrance, with its decoration, its original furniture and its large gallery on the mezzanine, which is supported by ornate capitals decorated with gilded heads of oriental inspiration, will all be restored. The main façade, inspired by geometric Art Nouveau, has a domed bow window, which extends across two floors. Its top is pieced with the elongated oculi that are so typical of the Viennese Secession style. A balcony with a stone balustrade adds a finishing touch. The façade features a gable, on which a rooster, the logo of the Pathé company, stands. Take a short detour past 28, Rue Van Praet to find the secondary entrance. Its geometric style already heralds Art Deco.

At no. 5–9 Rue du Lombard, we walk past an apartment building with stores on the ground floor, which Paul Hamesse built in 1908. The geometric Art Nouveau façade, with its visible metal structure, has a set of two trapezoidal oriels (listed on 3 June 1993). During this walk, we will see how easily Paul Hamesse could switch from one design to another. At the same time, we will also have plenty of time to reflect on how fragile these buildings are and on the fact that their owners should show them a little more love.

At no. 30–32 Rue du Lombard, on the corner with Rue de l'Étuve, you will see a nice corner building. The ground floor storefront and basement were renovated in 1952. This building, which was designed in 1909, is typical of the style of Paul Vizzavona, an architect who reconciled Art Nouveau with French classicism. Here the classic influences are apparent in the natural stone he used for the façade, as well as in the roof with its attic rooms and the overall sense of harmony of the design (listed on 22 December 2005).

6/ COMMEMORATIVE PLAQUE FOR CHARLES BULS

CORNER OF GRAND-PLACE AND RUE CHARLES BULS

Architect: Victor Horta; sculptor: Victor Rousseau
1899

If you thought there were no traces of Art Nouveau in Grand-Place, think again! This monument, which is located near the recumbent effigy of Everard t'Serclaes (sculptor Julien Dillens, 1902), was designed by the architect Victor Horta together with the sculptor Victor Rousseau, two protagonists of Art Nouveau. It paid tribute to Charles Buls (1837–1914), who served as mayor from 1881 until 1899, and was a token of gratitude for services to artists and for his major role in the city's conservation.

To the left, a seated young woman meditates. Holding a compass, and an unfolded plan, she pays tribute to the architects who helped build Grand-Place from the fifteenth to the seventeenth century.

In the centre, a young man holds a burning oil lamp, the symbol of light. He is standing on a structure in which one can recognise Victor Horta's typical whiplash design, made of acacia branches that blend in with the decoration.

Charles Buls, Victor Horta and Victor Rousseau were all members of Les Amis Philanthropes, the Grand Orient lodge of Belgium. You can also interpret the monument in light of the mayor's sympathies and philosophical

convictions. In addition to the tools of the architect's trade, the compass that the young woman holds can also be seen as a symbol of moderation which must be preserved at all times and the quest for perfection, which are both masonic principles.
The adolescent is an allegory of the beginning of the esoteric quest, while acacia branches, a symbol of immortality, refer to the legend of Master Hiram, the architect of Solomon's Temple, who was murdered by bad companions and whose grave was found in the desert thanks to the acacia that flowered there.[4]

If the shutters are open at 7, Rue de la Madeleine, you will have the opportunity to admire the striking storefront of Marjolaine, which was designed by Léon Sneyers in 1904. It demonstrates how prosperous this shopping street used to be in the early twentieth century and is a very interesting example of the geometric Art Nouveau style. It has been restored with great care. This very small work nonetheless marks an important turning point in the career of Sneyers, who emulated Paul Hankar's style. It points to the architect's transition to a more refined and abstract style, influenced by the Viennese Secession, which would go on to become his trademark (listed on 18 December 1997).

7/ OLD ENGLAND DEPARTMENT STORE MUSICAL INSTRUMENTS MUSEUM (MIM)

RUE MONTAGNE DE LA COUR 2, 1000 BRUSSELS

Architect: Paul Saintenoy
1898
Listed: 30 March 1989

The Old England brand, which could be found across Europe, specialised in the sale of fashionable items and British food specialities. It opened a branch in Brussels in 1886. The Brussels branch was expanded several times. As a result, it occupied the entire block between place Royale and Rue Villa Hermosa. The most spectacular extension was built in 1898–1899, on the corner of Rue Montagne de la Cour and Rue Villa Hermosa, by the architect Paul Saintenoy together with the architect Jules De Becker (1847–1906).
As a result, Old England became the go-to department store for the latest items, selling a vast array of goods on six floors. A lift took customers up to the tea room on the top floor, which also had a panoramic terrace.
By the Thirties, Art Nouveau was no longer considered fashionable, which is why the building underwent some alterations. The metal façade was stripped of all its iron and cast iron decorations and painted white. In 1956, the corner turret was dismantled. By the end of the Sixties, the store moved to Avenue Louise. The building was sold in 1973 and used as sales premises by a rug store. In 1979, the Belgian state acquired the building for the Musical Instruments Museum. The restoration was undertaken in 1989, also including the adjoining building, a neoclassical mansion on the corner of Place Royale. The museum opened in June 2000. The Art Nouveau building is now mainly used for the museum displays. The collections are kept in the neighbouring building. The landings around the stairwell and lift are occupied by the reception, a bookshop, and an exhibition gallery which focuses on the building's history and its architect, Saintenoy. A brasserie opened on the sixth floor. You can visit all these spaces for free when the museum is open.
The façade of the Old England building was revolutionary. It inspired the renovation of the design of many a department store in Brussels. Even Victor Horta was inspired by it when he designed the Innovation. The

completely transparent façade is built around a fine metal structure, with large glazed windows that let in plenty of light. The structure is enhanced by plenty of railings (facilitating the cleaning of the windows) and exuberant decorative bars. At the corner of the building, a particularly expressive turret stands out, which was added during the restoration, as does the large awning at the entrance. Many of the porcelain stoneware elements, including the large sign and the many coats of arms, were produced by Vermeren-Coché of Ixelles.

The interior has retained many of its decorative elements, which were restored or recreated, including the mosaic floors on the ground floor and the stencilled paintings on the beams and ceilings representing thistle or chestnut leaves. The decorative cast iron elements that were attached to the upper part of the pillars have been restored based on a few rare copies that were preserved. The stairwell and lift were partially changed.

Paul Saintenoy (1862–1952) was born into a family of architects and was a key figure in Brussels architecture in the 1900s. His desire to reconcile the enhancement of the vestiges of the past with a new architecture based on the forms and techniques of his time gave rise to a style that combined neo-Renaissance, eclectic and Art Nouveau elements. This is perfectly illustrated in his projects in the Montagne de la Cour neighbourhood. Here Saintenoy restored sixteenth-century mansions (at no. 1 and 3 in Rue Ravenstein). Here he also built the Delacre Pharmacy in the Flemish neo-Renaissance style (at no. 62–66 Coudenberg) and where he designed the extension of the Old England department store in the Art Nouveau style.

8/ HÔTEL GRESHAM AND MUSEUM FIN-DE-SIÈCLE MUSEUM

PLACE ROYALE 3, 1000 BRUSSELS

Classement: 21 octobre 1993

At 3, Place Royale, a neoclassical building dating from the end of the eighteenth century, serves as the entrance to the Museum of Fine Arts (and the brasserie and museum shop). It has retained its Art Nouveau interior decorative scheme, which was designed by Léon Govaerts in 1900–1901. The design was commissioned by the Gresham Life Assurance Society Limited, a British life insurance company founded in London in 1848, which became the owner of the building in 1900. In 1967, the Belgian state bought the building so the Museum of Fine Arts could be extended. It was restored between 1999 and 2003 and features mosaic floors, stained glass, sgraffiti, electric lamps, letterboxes, and so on.The centrepiece, without a doubt, is the white marble staircase veined with grey, surrounded by curved walls with stained glass and sgraffiti, which leads to the brasserie.

Don't forget to visit the Fin-de-Siècle Museum, which was inaugurated in December 2013, and which evokes the capital's vibrant arts scene during the years from 1868 until 1914. It exhibits works by plenty of Art Nouveau artists including Constantin Meunier, James Ensor, Henri Evenepoel, and Fernand Khnopff. At the same time, it also focuses on other art disciplines, including literature, music, photography, and architecture.

The museum also showcases the prestigious Gillion Crowet Collection, which Baron and Baroness Gillion Crowet amassed from the 1960s onwards, at a time when Art Nouveau was no longer deemed relevant. It comprises over 230 works from this amazing era, bearing witness to the encounter between the fine arts and the decorative arts around 1900. This collection is very comprehensive, touching upon the close exchanges between Brussels, Paris and Nancy. Artists featured in the collection include Majorelle, Gallé, Mucha, Wolfers, and Horta...

▼ Entrance Hall of the Gresham Hotel (Museum of Fine Arts)

PLACES TO SEE

- **Hôtel Solvay** – www.hotelsolvay.be
- **Maison Autrique** – www.autrique.be
- **Musée de la BD** – www.cbbd.be
- **Maison Cauchie** – www.cauchie.be
- **Musée Charlier** – www.charliermuseum.be
- **Cinquantenaire Museum and Pavilion of the Human Passions** (or Horta-Lambeaux pavilion) – www.kmkg-mrah.be
- **Musée Fin-de-Siècle Museum** – www.fin-de-siecle-museum.be
- **Musée Horta** – www.hortamuseum.be
- **Musical instruments museum** – www.mim.be
- **Train World** – www.trainworld.be

HERITAGE CONSERVATION AND AWARENESS

- **Monuments and Sites Directorate**
  www.patrimoine.brussels
- **Pétitions-Patrimoine ASBL**
  petitionspatrimoine.blogspot.be
- **VZW Homegrade.Brussels ASBL** –
  www.centreurbain.be
  Information centre Halles Saint-Géry - Place Saint-Géry 1, 1000 Brussels
- ***Les Nouvelles du Patrimoine***
  www.nouvellesdupatrimoine.be
  Journal of the Friends of UNESCO in Belgium
- **APEB** – Association for the Study of Built Heritage
  www.apeb-vsg.be
- **GERPM-SC** – Study and research group for murals – cultural sgraffito works - Rue des Champs-Élysées 72, 1050 Ixelles

GUIDED VISITS AND EVENTS

- **Cécile Dubois**
  cecile8968@hotmail.com
  Phone: 0478 229 228
- **Explore.brussels asbl**
  www.explore.brussels
  The umbrella association of ARAU, Arkadia, Brussels Chatterguides, and Pro Velo regularly organises the Brussels Art Nouveau & Art Deco Festival (BANAD festival).
- **Festival ARTONOV ASBL**
  www.festival-artonov.eu
  Interdisciplinary festival (music, dance, theatre, visual arts, and fashion) inspired by Art Nouveau and Art Deco.

WEBSITES ABOUT ART NOUVEAU HERITAGE

- www.irismonument.be – Inventory of the architectural heritage of the Brussels-Capital Region and registers of listed heritage sites
- www.artnouveau-net.eu – Réseau Art nouveau Network
- www.villedarchitectes.brussels – Brussels, city of architects
- www.gustavestrauven.brussels – Website about the architect Gustave Strauven
- www.paulhamesse.brussels – Website about the architect Paul Hamesse
- www.bruciel.brussels – BruCiel
  This app can be used to simultaneously view aerial photos from two different periods, from the early Thirties until 2014.

DOCUMENTATION CENTRE

The CIVA Foundation – www.fondationciva.brussels
The CIVA Foundation develops a wide array of events and services including temporary and permanent exhibitions, conferences, and educational activities and events. It makes available an exceptional array of archives and libraries to the public, containing just under 40,000 works and journals on architecture, town planning, the history of cities, landscapes, gardens and urban ecology.

BIBLIOGRAPHY

Websites:

- Inventory of architectural heritage: www.irismonument.be
- Listing decree: http://patrimoine.brussels/liens/registre/registre-du-patrimoine-protege-en-region-de-bruxelles-capitale-liste

General information

- Collectif, *Dictionnaire des femmes belges. XIXe et XXe siècles*, Brussels, Racine, 2006
- *Itinéraire de la Franc-Maçonnerie à Bruxelles*, Brussels, Royal Belgian Geographical Society and Parcours maçonnique, 2008 (collection Hommes et Paysages, n° 31)
- S. Jaumain (dir.), *Dictionnaire d'Histoire de Bruxelles*, Brussels, Prosopon, 2013

General works on architecture in Belgium and Brussels

- *Académie de Bruxelles. Deux siècles d'architecture*, Brussels, AAM, 1989
- I. Biver, *Cinémas de Bruxelles. Portraits et destins*, Brussels, CFC-Éditions, 2009
- Collectif, *Le Patrimoine monumental de la Belgique. Bruxelles*, 3 tomes, Liège, Mardaga, 1989-1994
- Cooparch-RU, *Les Sites remarquables du patrimoine social bruxellois*, Brussels, Société du logement de la Région bruxelloise, 2000
- G. De Hens et V.-G. Martiny, *Académie royale des Beaux-Arts de Bruxelles, une école d'architecture, des tendances*, Brussels, Société populaire d'éditions, 1992
- *Itinéraire du patrimoine résidentiel bruxellois*, Brussels, Société royale belge de géographie, 2007 (collection Hommes et Paysages, n° 38-39)
- *Le Foyer Schaerbeekois. 100 ans*, Brussels, Les Dossiers de La Fonderie, 1999
- A. Van Loo (dir.), *Dictionnaire de l'architecture en Belgique de 1830 à nos jours*, Antwerp, Fonds Mercator, 2003

General works on Art Nouveau in Brussels

- *L'Académie et l'Art nouveau. 50 artistes autour de Victor Horta*, 2 tomes, Brussels, Les Amis de l'Académie, 1996
- Fr. Borsi et H. Wieser, *Bruxelles, capitale de l'Art nouveau*, Braine-l'Alleud, J.-M. Collet, 1996
- G. Conde-Reis (dir.), *Flora's Feast. Le motif floral dans l'Art nouveau*, Brussels, Brussels-Capital Region, 2015
- Collectif, *Les Sgraffites à Bruxelles*, Brussels, Fondation Roi Baudouin, 1996
- Collectif, *Encyclopédie de l'Art nouveau, tome I, Le Quartier Nord-Est à Bruxelles*, Brussels, Centre d'information, de documentation et d'étude du patrimoine (CIDEP), 1999
- M. Culot et Fr. Terlinden, *Antoine Pompe et l'effort moderne en Belgique. 1890-1940*, Brussels, Éditions du Musée d'Ixelles, 1969
- Ch. Declève, *Guide des décors céramiques à Bruxelles de 1880 à 1940*, Brussels, Declève et Alberty, 1996
- B. Schoonbroodt, *Artistes belges de l'Art nouveau – 1890-1914*, Brussels, Racine, 2008

Works about a specific architect or building

- J. Arets, *Ernest Blerot, architecte Art nouveau bruxellois. Un style, une ville. Monographie – Catalogue raisonné*, Brussels, Arets Galleries, 2013
- Fr. Aubry, *Horta ou la passion de l'architecture*, Ghent, Ludion, 2005
- Fr. Aubry, *Le Musée Horta. Saint-Gilles. Bruxelles*, Ghent, Ludion, 2001
- Fr. Blomme, *À la rencontre d'Adrien Blomme 1878-1940, sa vie son œuvre*, Brussels, CIVA, 2004

- Fr. Borsi et P. Portoghesi, *Victor Horta*, Brussels, Marc Vokar, 1990
- Collectif, *Hankar et l'hôtel Ciamberlani. Un palais déguisé en maison de ville*, Brussels, Aparté/Day Off, 2009
- Collectif, *Henry van de Velde. Passion, Fonction, Beauté*, Tielt, Lannoo, 2013
- Collectif, *La Maison Cauchie. Entre rêve et réalité*, Brussels, La Maison Cauchie, 2005
- Collectif, *Le Musée Charlier et Victor Horta. 1890-1893*, Brussels, AAM, 2012
- G. Conde-Reis (dir.), *Victor Horta – Hôtel Aubecq*, Brussels, Brussels-Capital Region, 2011
- « Dossier Jean-Baptiste Dewin », dans *Bruxelles Patrimoines*, n° 10, Brussels, Brussels-Capital Region, spring 2014, pp. 6-91
- M. Goslar, *Hôtel Hallet. Signé Horta*, Waterloo, Avant-Propos, 2011
- M. Goslar, *Victor Horta. 1861-1947. L'homme, l'architecte, l'Art nouveau*, Brussels, Fondation Lahaut/Fonds Mercator, 2012
- V. Horta, *Mémoires*, Brussels, Ministry of the French-speaking Community, 1985
- Fr. Jurion-de Waha et A. Wachtelaer, *Le petit monde de l'architecte Henri Jacobs. 1864-1935*, Brussels, Royal Brussels Archaeological Society, 2013
- Fr. Levie, *L'homme qui voulait classer le monde. Paul Otlet et le Mundaneum*, Brussels, Les Impressions nouvelles, 2006
- Fr. Loyer, *Dix ans d'Art nouveau. Paul Hankar. Architecte*, Brussels, CFC-Éditions/AAM, 1991
- L. Ploegaerts et P. Puttemans, *L'œuvre architecturale de Henry van de Velde*, Brussels – Québec, Atelier Vokaer – Les Presses de l'Université Laval, 1987
- B. Schoonbroodt, *Privat Livemont. Entre tradition et modernité au cœur de l'Art nouveau, 1861-1936*, Brussels, Racine, 2007

INDEX OF NAMES OF PERSONS

The pages to which you should refer for comprehensive biographical information are displayed in bold.

NOTES

Walk 1

1. V. Horta, *Mémoires*, Ministry of the French-speaking Community, Brussels, 1985,p. 65.
2. *Ibid.*
3. *Ibid.*, p. 68.
4. This manuscript was published in 1985 by the Ministry of the French-speaking community, under the supervision of Cécile Dulière.
5. P. Otlet, *Traité de Documentation – Le livre sur le Livre*, 1934 quoted in Fr. Levie, *L'homme qui voulait classer le monde. Paul Otlet et le Mundaneum*, Bruxelles, Les Impressions nouvelles, Brussels, 2006, p. 275.
6. V. Horta, *Mémoires*, Brussels, Ministry of the French-speaking Community, Brussels, 1985, p. 77.
7. *Ibid.*, p. 20.
8. *Ibid.*, p. 313.
9. The Arts and Crafts movement is a reformist art movement in the disciplines of architecture, the decorative arts, painting, and sculpture, which originated in Great Britain in the 1860s and developed in the 1880s and 1890s. It is considered the forerunner of Art Nouveau.
10. Charles Rennie Mackintosh (1868–1928) was a British architect and artist, and a member of the Arts and Crafts movement. He was the main proponent of Art Nouveau in Glasgow.

Walk 2

1. P. Puttemans, « L'œuvre d'Antoine Pompe », dans *Antoine Pompe et l'effort moderne en Belgique. 1890-1940*, Brussels, Éditions du Musée d'Ixelles, 1969, p. 21.
2. V. Horta, *Mémoires*, Brussels, Ministry of the French-speaking Community, 1985, p. 94.
3. J. Arets, *Ernest Blerot. Architecte Art nouveau bruxellois. Un style, une ville*, Brussels, Arets Galleries, 2013, p. 236.
4. M. Goslar, *Victor Horta 1861-1947, L'homme, l'architecte, l'Art nouveau, Bruxelles*, Fondation Pierre Lahaut and Fonds Mercator, 2012, pp. 59 et 491.
5. On Jean-Baptiste Dewin and the restoration of his private home, see 'Dossier Jean-Baptiste Dewin', in Bruxelles Patrimoines, no. 10,Brussels-Capital Region, Brussels, spring 2014, pp. 6–91.

Walk 3

1. Fr. Aubry, *Maisons sises* à *Saint-Gilles, 246-256 chaussée de Waterloo*, unpublished historical paper, Brussels, 1992.
2. V. Horta, *Mémoires*, Brussels, Ministry of the French-speaking Community, 1985, p. 44.
3. *Ibid.*
4. Listing decree of 8 June 2006.
5. www.bruxelles.be/artdet.cfm?id=6332&highlight=almanach
6. A.-C. Huwart, 'À 80 ans, l'auteur d'*Au nom de tous les miens* s'installe à Bruxelles. Le Modern Style éblouit Martin Gray', *Le Soir*, 13 mars 2002, p. 17.

Walk 4

1. www.motsetmuses.be.ma
2. The relief *Les Passions humaines* was initially named *Le Calvaire de l'humanité.*
3. www.apeb-vsg.be
4. www.wardeadregister.be/fr/content/strauven-1
5. V. Horta, *Mémoires*, Ministry of the French-speaking Community, Brussels, 1985, p. 307.
6. *Ibid.*, p. 77.
7. *Ibid.*, p. 78.
8. *Ibid.*.
9. *Ibid.*, p. 79.

Walk 5

1. V. Horta, *Mémoires*, Ministry of the French-speaking Community, Brussels, 1985, p. 87.

Walk 6

1. Fr. Jurion-de Waha et A. Wachtelaer, Le *petit monde de l'architecte Henri Jacobs. 1864-1935*, Brussels Archaeological Society, Brussels, 2013, p. 55.

Walk 7

1. V. Horta, *Mémoires*, Ministry of the French-speaking Community, Brussels, 1985, p. 31.
2. Fr. Jurion-de Waha et A. Wachtelaer, *Le petit monde de l'architecte Henri Jacobs. 1864-1935*, Brussels Archaeological Society, Brussels, 2013, p. 223.
3. Robert Schuiten (1912–1997) worked as an architect from the end of World War II until 1972.
4. Luc Schuiten is a visionary architect, who is passionate about the principle of 'archiborescence', a term he invented to designate architecture that uses living organisms to build vegetal cities.

Walk 8

1. V. Horta, *Mémoires*, Ministry of the French-speaking Community, Brussels, 1985, p.40.
2. *Ibid.*, p. 42.

Walk 9

1. *Ibid.*, p. 120.
2. *Ibid.*, p. 121.
3. *Ibid.*.
4. *Itinéraire de la Franc-Maçonnerie à Bruxelles*, collection Hommes et Paysages no. 31, Royal Belgian Geographical Society and Parcours Maçonnique, Brussels, 2008, pp. 44–45.

PHOTO CREDITS

Photos by Sophie Voituron
www.sophie-voituron.com

Except: Cécile Dubois: page 77 (bottom), 99 (bottom), 155- ©Gleamlight - Edificio: page 63 - ©Geneviève van Tichelen: page 117 - ©Commune of Schaerbeek / House of the Arts: page 127 - www.irismonument.be © SPRB – GOB: page 100, 128, 129 (top), 134 and 164 - ©phvercheval: page 75 (photo of the Dessicy family) - ©Claire Fontaine: page 20 - ©KMKG-MRAH: page 75 (The Mysterious Sphynx) - Vers l'Art, 1909, pl. 27, from www.irismonument.be: page 98 - ©Sofam 2018: Joseph Diongre: page 133 - Collection cartes postales de Belfius - Académie royale de Belgique: p. 150.

The authors wish to thank their entourage for their support during this project including Editions Racine, in particular Mrs Brutsaert and Mrs Poskin, for their trust and assistance, as well as Catherine Meeùs for her attentive proofreading and Catherine Chronopoulou for the graphic design.
They also wish to thank those individuals who graciously accepted to be interviewed for their portrait in this book, i.e., Mrs Aubry, Mrs Dessicy and Mrs Fontaine, as well as Mr Berckmans, Mr Metzger and Mr Schuiten.

Thanks also go to Tania Maamary (Edificio), Alexandra Rolland (Maison Autrique), Isabelle Bastaits (Museum of Fine Arts), Caroline Berckmans (APEB), Simone De Boeck (GERPM-SC), Anne-Cécile Maréchal (Commune of Schaerbeek), Geneviève van Tichelen, Dominique de Thibault and Michel Wittamer (Hôtel Solvay), Anne-Sophie Buffat (Réseau Art Nouveau Network), Philippe Bovy (Urban planning department of the Commune of Ixelles), Tom Verhofstadt (Monuments and Sites Directorate), Olga and Michel Gilbert, Claude Delhaye, Werner Adriaenssens and Denis Perrin (KMKG-MRAH).
Thank you finally to all those who contribute daily to the conservation of our very fragile and valuable Art Nouveau heritage.

Cover caption:
Top: Nursery, Rue Saint-Ghislain 40, 1000 Brussels, Victor Horta, 1895
Bottom: Sgraffito of Maison Cauchie, Rue des Francs 5, 1040 Etterbeek, Paul Cauchie, 1904–1905

Text: Cécile Dubois
Translation from French: Sandy Logan
Proofreading: Jonathan Michaelson
Photos: Sophie Voituron
Layout and maps: Aikaterini Chronopoulou • www.aika-design.com

For more information:
www.racine.be
Subscribe to our newsletter to receive regular updates about our publications and activities.

Tour et Taxis, Entrepôt royal
86C, avenue du Port, BP 104A • B - 1000 Brussels

D. 2018. 6852.3
Legal deposit: March 2018
ISBN 978-2-39025-045-6

Printed in Poland